Effective Women's Ministry

in the 21st Century

Effective Women's Ministry

in the 21st Century

Dr. Dee Klaus

VISION PUBLISHING
Ramona, California

Copyright 2004

All rights are reserved internationally
except for brief comments in articles, etc.
and only by permission of the author.

ISBN: 1-931178-56-9
Copyright, Delores Klaus, 2004

Vision Publishing
1520 Main Street, Suite C
Ramona, CA 92065
www.visionpublishingservices.com

Scriptures are taken from the
New King James Bible
and the Amplified Bible
unless otherwise stated.

Acknowledgments

Many people have played an important role in creating this handbook, and I am very grateful for their inputs, suggestions, and encouragement along my journey to complete this enormous project.

- Dr. Stan DeKoven, President of VICU, for his inspiration, encouragement, and confidence in the end results of this book.
- Dr. Kluane Spake, founder of Sword Inc. for her scholarly, reliable, spirit-filled, and serious examination of the Biblical concept of headship
- Pastor Cathy Guerrero, co-pastor with her husband, Dr. Jason of Regency Christian Center Int'l, who conducts monthly Life Builders Seminars for future women leaders. The impact of her teaching has opened my thinking to a new concept of leadership development for today's world.
- Dr. Pat Hulsey, co-founder of Harvestime International Network, who is a prolific writer, educator, and mentor for many world leaders, and humbly supports the Women's Studies Degree Program for VICU with her in-depth women's courses.
- Pastor Diane Gardner, Senior Pastor of Inheritance Family Life Church, who has persevered in the trials women ministers face in today's society. She has been such a testimony and encouragement to me in her diligent pursuit of God's calling.

Many kudos and grateful thanks to so many unsung heroines in women's ministry whom I have learned from and who, along the way, have touched hundreds of women's lives through their labor and contributions to developing women's ministries.

Special thanks to my prayer partners, Eunice Welsh, Lavonne Wilhoite, and Victoria Cannon, who are my cheerleaders and warriors in His works.

Finally, many thanks to my husband, Tal, for his support in reviewing and editing this work, and his confidence and unending love.

DEDICATION

This book is dedicated to all the women who are praying about starting a women's ministry, to those struggling through some of the start-up bumps in the road, and to those whose ministries are thriving and making a difference in the lives of their members, their church body, and to the community. I'd also like to dedicate this book to the "Women of Destiny" of Summit Christian Church, San Marcos, CA, who have supported and encouraged me in our prayer groups, conferences, special events, and other outreaches.

TABLE OF CONTENTS

Forewords	9
Prologue	13
Part I: A Biblical & Practical Model for Women's Ministry	15
Chapter 1 *How to Begin to Create the Nucleus*	19
Chapter 2 *Develop a Philosophy*	25
Chapter 3 *Planning & Developing a Balanced Ministry*	37
Chapter 4 *Ways to Implement Ministry*	49
Part II: Training, Preparation, & Motivation	57
Chapter 5 *Building Your Leadership Team*	61
Chapter 6 *Tools to Help Women Discover Their Call & Gifts*	69
Part III: Disciple & Develop Leadership	83
Chapter 7 *Effective Christian Foundational Training*	87
Chapter 8 *Understanding Historical Views of Women's Roles*	111
Chapter 9 *Developing Pulpit Ministry Leadership*	139
Part IV: Evangelism & Outreaches	161
Chapter 10 *Women's Community Outreaches*	165
Chapter 11 *Conferences & Retreats*	179
Chapter 12 *Prison Ministry & Re-entry Programs*	189
Part V: Run Toward the Goal	203
Chapter 13 *Women's Ministry that Makes the Difference*	207
Epilogue	221
Appendices	223
1 *Sample Brochure for Women's Ministry*	225
2 *Motivational Gifts Test*	227
3 *Sample Brochure for Conference/Retreat*	235
4 *Sample Conference/Retreat Timeline*	237
5 *Sample Conference/Retreat Budget*	239
6 *Recommended Reading for Women's Ministry*	241

FOREWORD
Mrs. Gordon (Freda) Lindsay

When Dr. Yongi Cho, a pastor in Seoul Korea, noticed that over half of the "troops" in his church were women (un-enlisted), he decided to take action: put them to work! He soon realized that some of his best leaders were women. Today, he pastors the world's largest known congregation in Christendom, Yoido Full Gospel Church, with a membership of 780,000.

Never before, in the history of the world, have women had such opportunities to fill key positions – some for good and some for evil. There was Golda Meir, a prime minister during one of Israel's crucial wars; Margaret Thatcher in Britain; Indira Gandhi in India. While serving as governor of Texas, George W. Bush invited some 20 ministers from throughout the U.S. to a gathering in Dallas. I was surprised to be the only woman present. Governor Bush shared his personal testimony with our group stating that when his father was president, Billy Graham had visited the Bush family home, and while there, took a walk with George W., discussing spiritual matters. It was this talk that was instrumental in George W. later receiving Jesus as his Savior.

Governor Bush concluded his speech by inviting questions from the ministers in attendance. After several men spoke up, I followed by asking if he should become president how he would treat Israel, and would he select qualified women to key positions in his cabinet. To the first, he answered, "I will always be Israel's friend, as she is the only democratic nation in that part of the world, and we need friends." To the second question, he stated that he would select loyal, well-trained women. He did, and Condoleezza Rice was recently appointed Secretary of State. Karen Hughes writes some of his speeches and often travels with him to important meetings. President Bush's wife, Laura, is a fine example to the women of America and the world.

The Christian nations give a marvelous advantage to women while the Islamic and other heathen countries make slaves out of many of their women.

My late husband, Gordon, used to say, "Show me how a man/woman uses their leisure time, and I'll show you what they will accomplish in life – whether it is to win souls to the Lord if they are believers, or waste their future if they are unbelievers."

Dr. Dee Klaus has just finished an awesome new book, *Effective Women's Ministry in the 21st Century*! In great and interesting detail, she carefully tells a woman how to plow, pray for and set in motion a successful women's ministry in the church and the community. Some of the topics discussed in her book are: parenting, healing wounded women, ministering to women and girls in prison, retreats, conventions, talent shows and dance groups for special times. She carefully defines Greek and Hebrew words, correctly translating the gender of certain words. Her book also contains the testimonies of 10 prominent Christian women in leadership roles. Dr. Klaus covers it all; nothing is overlooked.

Both the Old and New Testament Scriptures honor women:

> "The Lord gives the command; The women who proclaim the good tidings are a great host (Psalm 68:11 NAS)."

> "Now after He had risen early on the first day of the week, He first appeared to Mary Magdalene, from whom He had cast out seven demons (Mark 16:9 NAS)."

After His resurrection, Jesus first appeared to women at the tomb. He told both men and women to go into all the world and preach the Gospel. Women were also in the Upper Room when the Holy Spirit was poured out in Acts 2:4, including Jesus' mother, Mary. *Effective Women's Ministry in the 21st Century* can and should change the lives of multitudes of women who will open their hearts to hear what God is saying through Dr. Dee Klaus.

Mrs. Gordon (Freda) Lindsay

FOREWORD

By Dr. Kluane Spake

From the beginning, God's creation plan was for "both men and women" to rule in dominion and manifest His likeness and image (Gen. 1-26-28). Joel cried out this intention, "… I will pour out my Spirit on all people. Your sons and daughters will prophesy… (both men and women.)… I will pour out my Spirit in those days (Joel 2:28-29 NIV). Paul emphasized this expectation when he said, "We are no longer… merely men or women, but we are all the same – we are Christians; we are one in Christ Jesus" (Gal 3:28 TLB).

My effort over many years was to establish the Biblical truth that it was God's plan for women to be equal participants at home as well as in ministry to the nations. God did call all humanity to be ONE – and that's Good News! When translated correctly, we can clearly ascertain from Scripture that Paul did vitally support women in ministry. Furthermore, significant Christian women have historically influenced and helped shape our present world.

With those truths of equality firmly in mind, my friend, Dr. Dee Klaus, has put her efforts into researching some of the best ideas on how to establish effective women's ministries in the local church setting. Not only do women need the truth of equality, but they also need to be equipped, trained, and mentored to lead.

There are other books about ministry out there -- this one is about "effectiveness." In this inclusive presentation, Dr. Klaus gives us a model for ministry that works! I pray that you begin to implement many of these effectual ideas right away!

God's friend and yours –
Dr. Kluane Spake
www.kluane.org
spake@mindspring.com

Prologue

The desire to write a book on this subject originated with the need to develop a women's ministry book for the "Institute for Women's Studies" degree program for Vision International College and University. As the Dean of Women's Ministry at Vision, I found there was a limited amount of collective material geared to this subject. This lack was the catalyst for my writing this book to prepare women of the twenty-first century for effective women's ministries.

There is a desire today in the hearts of women to evangelize, disciple, and touch the lost and dying in our society. With all the distractions of life, from being a homemaker or a working woman to trying to balance hectic schedules of being a successful wife, mother, single parent or student, there seems to be no time left to seek the fulfillment of our spiritual lives.

Many surveys show a growing enthusiasm for women to pursue exercise and health habits, but little time or thought is put into the development of the soul and spirit. Health is needed in all three areas of life, body, soul, and spirit. Each area is important in living an overcoming Christian life.

Over the years, with my involvement in women's ministry in local church settings, I found many women gifted with untapped resources, but who struggled in their pursuit to find purpose and destiny. Many required tools to help build a lasting ministry. These include undeveloped skills in gender dynamics, foundational childhood beliefs, pulpit ministry and other issues pertinent to their mission field.

My heart empathizes with women who strive to develop a successful ministry in the church and community. I wanted to help by sharing my research and experience, setting forth a strategy for the development of successful women's ministry in the 21st century.

There is a need for women to be trained with a strong Biblical foundation to address issues they would be confronted with as leaders. If these fundamental beliefs are not taught to enable all the leaders to minister in unity with the same goals, there could be undesirable consequences for the ministry. Unity in the body of Christ at all levels is a very important element in developing tomorrow's leaders.

> *"His intention was the perfecting and the full equipping of the saints {His consecrated people}, {that they should do} the work of ministering toward building up Christ's body (the church), {That it might develop} until we all attain oneness in the faith and in the comprehension of the {full and accurate) knowledge of the Son of God that (we might arrive) at really mature manhood {the completeness of personality which is nothing less than the standard height of Christ's own perfection}, the measure of the stature of the fullness of the Christ and the completeness found in Him."*
> (*Ephesians 4:12-13, Amplified*),

Much of the material on any subject comes from past experiences, trial and error, thoughts and perceptions of what works(ed) for the author, based on what many others have tried and written about. Years of collecting information and weighing what was presented, along with planning and conducting various women's ministries, has resulted in a wealth of information useful for women's ministry. Although this work is intended to be used as a course in a Women's Studies program, it is also designed as a stand-alone guide to assist women in developing their ministries in their neighborhoods, churches, and community.

My hope and prayer is that, in the preparation of this book, many ministries will gain the tools needed to prepare an effective ministry to women in a productive and valuable time frame; it is so needed in today's world.

> *"The Lord gives the word of power; the women who bear and publish the news are a great host."* (Psalm 68:11, Amplified)

Blessings,
Dr. Dee Klaus

Part 1

A BIBLICAL & PRACTICAL MODEL
FOR
WOMEN'S MINISTRY

"For we are fellow workmen (joint promoters, laborers together) with and for God; you are God's garden and vineyard and field under cultivation, (you are) God's building."

(I Corinthians 3:9, Amplified)

PART I: A Biblical & Practical Model for Women's Ministry

In today's world there is a great need and compelling call from God to raise up modern day women to hear and respond to the "Great Commission" call for the lost and dying. The Apostle, prophet, evangelists, pastors, teachers (five-fold ministry) are contributors in developing a women's ministry. The concept of team ministry, planting women's ministry across the nation and world, should be a continuous on-the-job training experience. Components for a women's ministry will vary, because the Lord (Himself) must knit the team together.

(Romans 12:4:4-5, Amplified) "For as in one physical body we have many parts (organs, members) and all of these parts do not have the same function or use. So we, numerous, as we are, are one body in Christ (the Messiah) and individually we are parts one of another (mutually dependent on one another)."

As we pursue a Biblical and practical model for women's ministry there are numerous ideas, resources, and methods to consider, especially as we begin to review the myriad of issues that are involved in establishing the foundation for such a ministry. It's like looking at different blueprints and determining the construction steps needed to complete the task of building. As spiritual leaders we must always remember that **Christ is the master builder**.

In Part I of this book we look at some procedures pertinent to getting started on the journey to developing an effective and lasting women's ministry. In Part I we will discuss:

- How to Begin to Create the Nucleus of a Women's Ministry
- Developing a Philosophy For Women's Ministry
- Planning & Developing a Balanced Ministry to Women
- Looking at Ways to Implement Ministry to Women

First we must develop the Core or Nucleus

Chapter 1: *How to Begin to Create the Nucleus*

Usually the first question for one desiring to start a ministry is, "How do we get started?" The first step is to gather a group of committed women to pray for God's direction. If a ministry dedicated to God is to succeed, it must be birthed in the will of God. This can only come by prayer (and sometimes fasting). We need to hear collectively what God is saying to our hearts.

Along with prayer, brainstorming is a great way to begin the group process. Of course, these assembled must realize what brainstorming means. It is the unrestrained offering of ideas or suggestions by all members of a committee or group of people in an effort to generate fresh ideas. The plan is to generate many ideas without reservation of the accumulative evaluation in the process. There should be no restraints on the offering of constructive methods or ideas for review. Sometimes an idea from one will stimulate additional input from another, adding a more conclusive part of the nucleus. The following are guidelines to consider.

- Select women of different ages to insure that ideas are motivated by real circumstances germaine to their lives.
- Select women outside your sphere, so their input is not merely familiar ideas of the core group.
- Communicate effectively ideas and inputs of your vision, purpose and goals.
- Do not do all the evaluating of the ideas with a select few. Let others' comments be a part of the analysis submitted for the final evaluation.
- Instruct participants not to evaluate before all the ideas and inputs are communicated.

Questionnaires and surveys are great tools for evaluating the target of your ministry. It allows the participants to take time to evaluate their conclusions based upon the suggestions of the survey and to add other inputs. I would suggest that the team make a list of the women you give the survey to and place a time limit on when the questionnaire/surveys should be completed and returned. Figure 1.0 provides a sample Questionnaire/Survey available for your use and Figure 1.1 is a Questionnaire Survey Summary sample of 27 women's responses quantified for you.

(Title of your Women's Ministry)
Q u e s t i o n n a i r e - (SAMPLE)

We would like to become more acquainted with your vision of women ministry in our church (could put group name here). Please fill out and return the following questionnaire regarding (Group Name) Women's Ministry. The following is designed with suggestions for you, but we also would like your additional suggestions. Please rate your desires on a scale of 0-5, with 5 being the most desirous.

Women's Meetings: (Quarterly)
_____ Regular Meetings (Praise/Worship, Message and Ministry Time)
_____ Special Speakers – Outside the Church (Formatted as regular meeting)
_____ Celebration of Praise (Overcoming Testimonies, uplifting the group)
_____ Progressive Dinner (1 house – salad, next house – dinner, last house –dessert), ending with regular meeting.
_____ Fashion Show (Presenting fashions desired with special music, message)
_____ Tea Party (Favorite tea & special desserts to share) at regular meeting
_____ Talent Show (Songs, spiritual dance, musical instrument, poems)
_____ Mother/Daughter Banquet with a program designed to minister to mother and daughter.

Special Topics:
_____ Word of God Message: (such as)
_____ Prayer, _____ Spiritual Gifts, _____ Spiritual Warfare, _____ Forgiven, Other Suggestions _____
_____ Parenting (How to raise a child/teenager in a changing world)
_____ Marriage (Exploring how beliefs, ethnic and generational background can help or hinder us as women to live a fulfilling life).
_____ Healing the Wounded Women
_____ Women of the Bible
_____ Outreaches in our Community
(Finding out ways we can help our church community)

Retreats
_____ One Day, _____ Friday night and Saturday daytime,
_____ Friday night and Saturday (day & nights), plus Sunday to noon

Special Retreat Places (besides Palomar Mountain)
_____

OTHER SUGGESTIONS NOT LISTED:
_____
_____

Fill out this portion, if you would like to volunteer in any of these events listed above:

Name:_____ Telephone No._____
Event or Position: _____

Thank you for taking the time to fill out this questionnaire!

Figure 1.0 Questionnaire (Sample)

(Title of your Ministry)
Questionnaire – Summary - (SAMPLE)
SUMMARY RATING BY A SCALE OF 0 TO 5 WITH 5 BEING THE MOST DESIROUS

Women's Meetings (Quarterly)
4.38 (19)   Regular Meetings (Praise/Worship, Message and Ministering Time)
3.87 (15)   Special Speakers – Outside the Church (Formatted as regular meeting)
4.41 (17)   Celebration of Praise (Overcoming testimonies, uplifting the group)
3.59 (17)   Progressive Dinner (1 house – salad, next house – dinner, last house – dessert), ending with regular meeting.
3.24 (17)   Fashion Show (Presenting fashions desired) with special music, message.
3.89 (16)   Tea party (Favorite tea and special desserts to share) during regular meetings.
4.82 (17)   Mother/Daughter Banquet (Breakfast, lunch or dinner) with special program designed to minister to mother and daughter.

Special Matter:
4.59 (17)   Word of God Message: (such as)
            4.60 (10) Prayer, 4.50 (10) Spiritual Gifts, 4.30 (10) Spiritual Warfare, 4.44 (9) Forgiveness. Other suggestions: (1) How to Study God's Word, (1) Women in Ministry.
4.21 (14)   Parenting (Raising a child/teenager in a changing world with Biblical guidelines.
4.10 (15)   Marriage (Exploring how belies, ethnic and generational background can help or hinder us women to live a fulfilling life).
4.18 (17)   Healing the Wounded Woman
4.44 (18)   Women of the Bible
4.35 (17)   Outreaches in our Community (Ways we can help our church community)

Retreats:
4.00 (9) One Day, 4.33 (6) Friday night and Saturday daytime.
4.82 (11) 11) Friday night and Saturday (day & night), plus Sunday until noon

Special Retreat Places

(4) Big Bear, (3) Arrow Head, (3) Murrietta Hot Springs, (2) Beach House, (2) River Boats, (1) Yosemite, (1) Pine Valley, Calvary Chapel in Temecula, (1) Julian, (1) Alpine, (1) Catalina.

OTHER SUGGESTIONS NOT USED

(1) All Day Workshop, (1) Outreaches for Revival to break out, (1) Youth Rally, (1) All night prayer for our families, (1) Praise/Worship gathering, (1) Women's Home Fellowship.

Figure 1.1 Questionnaire Summary (Sample)

A Telephone Survey is another effective tool for gathering information. Sometimes a more personal touch interacting with women shows that you value their suggestions and participation in evaluating the vision for the women's ministry. Have a list of questions ready before calling, such as:

- We are conducting a pilot study for our women's ministry and would like to ask you what your interests are in this study.
- What is your preference in meeting times? (weekly, bi-monthy or monthly)
- What would you prefer the subject matter be about? (Word of God messages, women of the Bible, learning more about prayer, forgiveness, etc.)
- What would your suggestions be regarding conferences or retreats?
- Are you interested in small groups or intercessory prayer meetings? (groups such as: single moms, mothers with small babies, mothers with teenagers, husband/wife relationships, etc.)

It is much easier to have your questions ready before calling. Also, your callers should be trained and respect the participants' time.

When you have all your information available, take the time to select the elements that will constitute an effective women's ministry program. The following is a list of the common elements. [1]

a. Start with prayer	g. Build program on Bible study
b. Know your women	h. Have variety
c. Enlist church leadership	l. Provide support groups
d. Have specific goals	j. Have an outreach ministry
e. Have women lead the program	k. Encourage person friendships
f. Develop leadership among the women in the church body	l. Be flexible and relevant

After all the information is assembled and evaluated with ample prayer, you then begin to assess the programs. From polling many successful women's ministry programs around the country the consensus is:

a. Weekly meetings are more effective than bi-monthly or monthly meetings.
b. The main focus is more on Biblical Studies or Life Building Skills than missions or projects.
c. A variety of meetings with continuing evaluation is the foundation for growth.
d. A Board of the women's ministry should have a minimum time commitment and a maximum time for completed service. This ensures spiritual commitment is made before accepting leadership, and limits changing the Board of the women's ministry, so it doesn't become stagnant.

Once a nucleus is developed, the group must develop a philosophy for an effective women's ministry, which we will address in the next chapter.

References:
[1] Lucy Wood Malbery, Ph.D. (1996). *The Role of Women in Ministry.* Outreach, Inc.

End of Chapter Questions
Chapter 1

1. What are some guidelines to consider in the development of the nucleus of a women's ministry?
2. What is the importance of using a Questionnaire Survey or Telephone Survey for evaluating the needs to be addressed for such a ministry?
3. What are the elements that constitute an effective women's ministry?
4. In what order would you arrange the twelve elements that constitute an effective women's ministry?
5. Pick one of the twelve elements and elaborate how you would implement this task.

Chapter 2 *Develop a Philosophy*

In developing your philosophy, one of the first things you need to know is: "What does the Bible say about women?" In Genesis 1:26-31 God says:

"Let us make man in Our image, according to Our likeness; let them have dominion over the sea, over the birds of the air, and over the cattle, over all the earth and over every creeping thing that creeps on the earth. So God created man in His own image; in the image of God He created him; <u>male and female</u> He created them. Then God blessed them, and God said to them, 'Be fruitful and multiply; fill the earth and subdue it; have dominion over the fish of the sea, over the birds of the air, and over every living thing that moves on the earth.' And God said: 'See, I have given you every herb that yields seed which is on the face of all the earth, and every tree whose fruit yields seed to you it shall be for food. Also to every beast of the earth, to every bird of the air, in which there is life, I have given every green herb for food, and it was so. Then God saw everything that He had made, and indeed it was very good....'"

Gilbert Bilezikian, in his book "*Beyond the Sex Roles,*"[1] describes God's creation/design in a most conclusive way. He states that male/female sexual differentiation reflects realities contained with the very being of God, which are derived from Him as His image. Femaleness pertains to the image of God as fully as maleness. Although man and woman were created equal in nature they are also created different in function. They were created to share and be in harmony with each other. Creation and redemption qualified women for ministry. Galatians 3:28 tells us:

"There is neither Jew nor Greek, there is neither slave nor free, there is neither <u>male nor female</u>, for you are all one in Christ Jesus."

In regards to salvation, I Corinthians 12:7 tells us,

"But the manifestation of the Spirit is given to each one for the profit of all."

Women are qualified and equipped by redemption. Churches today have many ministries that are not mentioned in the Bible, but Scripture clearly mentions some of these ministries, which lay a foundation for ministry to women.

Ephesians 4:11-12 states,

> "....apostles, some prophets, some evangelists, and some pastors and teachers, for equipping of the saints for the work of ministry for the edifying of the body of Christ."

This Scripture tells us gifted people are to prepare people for God's work. Women are to be equipped to equip others for His service. Titus 2:3-5,

> "The older women likewise, that they be reverent in behavior, not slanderers, not given to much wine, teachers of good things, that they admonish the young women to love their husbands, to love their children, to be discreet, chaste, homemakers, good, obedient to their own husbands, that the word of God may not be blasphemed."

Women have no limits as to how they can serve and minister today. There are so many opportunities in women's ministries, outreaches, music, arts and drama. Families and churches are blessed by women's involvement in all areas of ministry. It is important to settle the issue of "What does the Bible says about women?" before we begin to develop a Biblical philosophy for women's ministry.

Ministry Development

Once you have determined that it is indeed God's will for women to minister (which I certainly hope you have), you must then develop the foundation of your work. In formatting your ministry, an important first step is to write the vision. Habakkuk 2:2,

> "Write the vision and make it plain on tablets, that he may run who reads it." (NKJ)

and the Amplified version says;

> "Write the vision and engrave it so plainly upon tablets that everyone who passes may be able to read it easily and quickly as he hastens by."

It is a good idea to make the vision plain, so everyone can catch the vision and run with it. The purpose statement of the ministry should confirm what the ministry is all about and what direction it is going. That way anyone reading it will know all about your purpose. Also, there should be goals developed for the ministry to keep the women stimulated and motivated. If your committee is involved in the development of your women ministry vision statement, purpose, and goals, they will rightly feel a part of it. This lends to giving the ministry full support and helps to promote the ministry. Illustrated below is a sample of a women's ministry vision statement, purpose and goals. This is a sample only. Each ministry needs to define their own purpose for existence based on the God-given vision placed in their hearts.

(Name of Ministry)

VISION

The vision of (Name of Ministry) Women's ministry is to seek to fulfill Christ's mission by encouraging women with a sense of belonging to God and each other, enabling women to become all they are to be in Christ, and equipping women for blessing others with the love, grace, and truth of Jesus Christ, while meeting the complex needs of today's woman.

"As each one has received a special gift, employ it in serving one another, as good stewards of the manifold grace of God. Whoever speaks, let him speak, as it were, the utterance of God; whoever serves, let him do so as by the strength which God supplies; so that in all things God may be glorified through Jesus Christ, to whom belongs the glory and dominion forever and ever." (I Peter 4:10, NAS)

PURPOSE

- To help produce the will of God in the lives of women.
- To maximize the potential of women's anointing, gifting and the revelation that God has for the fulfillment of their destiny.
- To train spiritual leaders to reach out to women, to bring them hope, healing, and reconciliation to God in a world that is crying out for help.
- To build God's influence in women's lives enabling them to touch their homes and families in a changing society filled with so many distractions from God's purpose for the family unit.
- To recognize and support the unity of the Spirit in the Body of Christ, so the world can know that we are His disciples.

GOAL

(Name of Ministry) Women's Ministry goal is to provide a safe environment where women can participate and become transformed into the image of God, be trained in the full potential of their calling and be used to train other women. The goal for women's ministry in our church is: *"As they grow and mature in godliness, they will be better equipped to nurture and serve in their families, to enrich the church, to evangelize their communities, and for those called, to be sent out to expand the kingdom of God living in other parts of our nation and the world."*

After developing your vision of purpose and goals, the next step is to set up your organization. A Women's Ministries Board needs to be selected. The size of your board will depend on the size of your ministry. Usually the pastor of the church selects a woman with organizational skills and with Christian maturity to serve as a director.

Sometimes the pastor's wife will oversee the ministry, but some pastor's wives do not want to be involved.. They are either co-pastoring the church or serving in other important functions of the church. Most of the time the director being selected is the woman who began the women's ministry by getting a group of women together, brainstorming ideas, and forming the nucleus. Usually, the Lord has given her a burden for the women's ministry.

Below is a model for establishing a Women's Ministry, organizationally. They include basic responsibilities, job descriptions and functions. This model has proven to be highly successful in beginning a women's ministry. The beauty of it is that it can later be expanded or modified.

ORGANIZATION
(Name of your Ministry)

Director	(Name)
Chairwomen:	
Decorations	(Name)
Hospitality	(Name)
Hostess	(Name)
Prayer Counselor	(Name)
Publicity	(Name)
Worship	(Name)
Drama/Dance	(Name)

Once you have names by these positions (some may by necessity be filled by the same leader), you then need to develop specific position descriptions.

(Women's Ministry Name)
Basic Responsibilities

MINISTRY CHAIRWOMAN'S QUALIFICATIONS
(Each Board Member receives a copy of this section)

Qualification of a serving ministry chairwoman are:

- Agree to serve a one-year term. Of course you must be...
- A born-again believer in Jesus and baptized in the Holy Spirit.
- A signed agreement with (Name of Ministry) statement of "What We Believe" is needed. (Be sure to have your belief statement ready to be signed.) This leader must be...
- Excited about women in ministry and desire to be part of it. Further, they must...
- Have a desire to be a servant (serving others), and have the discipline of...
- Daily Bible devotional reading, knowing basic foundations of the Bible, and a prayer time with intimate fellowship with the Lord. The leader must...
- Attend church regularly and participate in one of (Church name) home fellowships.
- A desire for leadership training and a willingness to participate in teamwork with others is essential.
- The approval of your husband, if married, is necessary along with an ....
- Ability to attend meetings regularly, while inputting recommendations regarding your area of ministry.
- A knowledge in praying with someone to receive Salvation in Christ and the Baptism of the Holy Spirit is needed. (A knowledge of deliverance ministry to set people free, if you are involved in an altar ministry, or prayer counseling during designated ministry times is helpful). Finally,...
- Attending leadership training provided by (Name of ministry) and encouraging your ministry workers to do the same is expected

DIRECTOR

The role of the director is to oversee the women's ministry under the direction of the Pastor over the women's Ministry............

(Continue writing a detailed job description that pertains to your ministry)

As a Director your requirements are:
- Believe and follow (Name of ministry) statement of "What We Believe."
- Encourage and strengthen Christian women in the community in their walk with the Lord.
- Keep the vision alive by keeping your purpose and goals in front of the women in ministry.
- Work in concert with your ministry chairwomen, under the direction of your pastor, to fine-tune all areas of ministry, including duty assignment, and to be available for advice and support.
- In unity, be a vital part of God's mighty plan of healing and restoring women.
- Work as a team to build relationships and fellowship, always taking into consideration the insights and recommendations of the ministry chairwomen.
- Always keep your focus on God, knowing our goals are centered on ministry to women, not on programs.

DECORATION CHAIRWOMAN

The role of the decoration chairwomen is to coordinate with the women's board under the direction of the Director of the women's ministry……..

(Continue writing a detailed job description that pertains to your ministry)

As a Decoration Chairwoman your requirements are:
- To agree with and follow the Ministry Chairwoman's Qualification.
- Select and arrange decorations for all meetings. Be sure to check with the Director and members of the committee sponsoring the event. The Decoration Chair is …..
- Required to have the decorations completed before the event begins, so that the surroundings will set the mood of cheerful expectation for when the guests arrive.
- If decorations are not to be used again for another event, try to sell them to someone, intending to raise money for the next event or finances for special projects.
- In order to avoid confusion of what to do with leftover decorations, be sure to remove them before cleaning the facility for the next event.
- In the event that you need to leave before the event is over, designate someone to complete your duties.

HOSPITALITY CHAIRWOMAN

The role of the hospitality chairwoman is to coordinate with the women's board under the direction of the Director of the women's ministry……..

(Continue writing a detailed job description that pertains to your ministry)

As a Hospitality Chairwoman your requirements are:

- To agree with and follow the Ministry Chairwoman's Qualification.
- Select and train servers. Recommend qualified women to the (Name of ministry) committee for approval.
- Arrive at the meeting early enough for hospitality setup. Check with the committee what the theme will be for the meeting and coordinate the refreshments appropriate for the event.
- Assign specific duties to each server. Use servers who are friendly, who enjoy people, and have a way of making women feel comfortable at the refreshment table or when serving individually at a table.
- Arrange for cleanup duty, so that the hospitality room or kitchen is ready for the next event.
- If there are leftover refreshments donated by volunteers ask them first if they want the leftovers. If they do not, distribute them to others before you leave.

HOSTESS CHAIRWOMAN

The role of the hostess chairwoman is to coordinate with the women's board under the direction of the Director of the women's ministry…………………

(Continue writing a detailed job description that pertains to your ministry)

As a Hostess Chairwoman your requirements are:

- To agree with and follow the Ministry Chairwoman's Qualification.
- Be an ambassador for Christ with His attributes, because you are the first woman the guests will encounter when arriving to the event. Select and train hostesses accordingly.
- Be sure to familiarize yourself with the facility, providing directions to the different areas, such as restrooms and workshop events.

- Assign specific duties to each hostess, such as; greeting women at the door, directing latecomers to open seats, collection of monies being charged for the event or serving as offering ushers.
- Be aware of the needs of the speaker, such as water and tissues.
- Arrange to set up the sound equipment, taping equipment, and child care if needed.

PRAYER COUNSELOR CHAIRWOMAN

The role of the prayer counselor chairwoman is to coordinate with the women's board under the direction of the Director of the women's ministry.

(Continue writing a detailed job description that pertains to your ministry)

As a Prayer Counselor Chairwoman your requirements are:

- To agree with and follow the Ministry Chairwoman's Qualification.
- Prayerfully select women as prayer counselors who are active in the Word of God and can minister God's Word.
- Keep in mind that prayer counseling is a petition for divine intervention. The length and type of prayer should depend on the receptivity of the women and the Holy Spirit's leading.
- Be aware when praying there should be a time of listening and for direction from the Lord. Expect the operation of the gifts of the Holy Spirit.
- Instruct your designated prayer counselors that prayer should be specific. Interview the person being prayed for to ascertain the person's needs before praying.
- It is essential to communicate hope to the one seeking help. Prayer counselors must have a spirit of hope, an expectation that the answer lies with God and that He will be faithful to express Himself through you as you pray.
- Remember, you are a prayer counselor, not a therapist. If person needs professional help, refer them to leadership for direction.

PUBLICITY CHAIRWOMAN

The role of the publicity chairwoman is to coordinate with the women's board under the direction of the Director of the women's ministry…………………..

(Continue writing a detailed job description that pertains to your ministry)

As a Publicity Chairwoman your requirements are:
- To agree with and follow the Ministry Chairwoman's Qualification.
- Mail out invitations with creative graphics that will stir interest for attending the events.
- When appropriate, make posters or brochures announcing the event, such as weekend conferences, retreats or one-day workshops that will serve as eye-catching ways to promote interest.
- Create an insert for the Sunday Church service summarizing the event(s) and testimonies of the women.
- Select and train volunteers to help you with the area-wide mailouts, putting publications together, follow-up phone calls, and help with any areas that are needed.

WORSHIP CHAIRWOMAN

The role of the worship chairwoman is to coordinate with the women's board under the direction of the Director of the women's ministry………………..

(Continue writing a detailed job description that pertains to your ministry)

As a Worship Chairman your requirements are:
- To agree with and follow the Ministry Chairwoman's Qualification.
- To express the purposes of the ministry of praise and worship because you are a worshipper who knows how to lead a group of women in worshipping the Lord.
- Demonstrate expressive worship as an outward expression of an inward emotion. This cannot be expressed through words alone, but through praise and worship.
- Demonstrate
- "Corporate Expression," how God wants His people to come together and corporately worship Him.

- Illustrate how God is moved by praise and worship to Him – how worship stirs up the heavenly realm. Ministers of praise and worship will stir up dormant areas in the lives of the women and bring them into a closer relationship with Him, "Face to Face."

DRAMA/DANCE CHAIRWOMAN

The role of the worship chairwoman is to coordinate with the women's board under the direction of the Director of the women's ministry………………..

(Continue writing a detailed job description that pertains to your ministry)

As a Drama/Dance Chairwoman your requirements are:

- To agree with and follow the Ministry Chairwoman's Qualification.
- To express the purposes of the ministry through drama/dance to illustrate the importance of the visual demonstration of a interpretation of the revelation of a prophetic message from the Lord.
- Teach others by showing that expressive dance is an outward expression of an inward emotion, that cannot be expressed through words alone, but through a dance company or solo dancers, with choreographic interpretations.
- Portray the character of God in dance – His faithfulness, His love, His fatherhood, His providence, and other attributes.
- Be responsible for the drama/dance team to insure integrity, commitment, obedience to God's will and dedication to the Lord in unity in heart, mind, and spirit.

This model provides some of the areas to cover in creating a ministry that will involve all areas of your vision. This model is a blueprint, designed to start building a lasting women's ministry, that will make a significant difference equipping women to serve in a church or community. Without a blueprint it is impossible to build the basic details involved in implementing a design, so the attempted project will not become an unsalvageable job because of much discouragement. This could happen in any ministry if the foundation is not set in order by God.

"For he waited expectantly looking forward to the city which has fixed and firm foundations, whose Architect and Builder is God." (Hebrews 11:10, Amplified)

References:

[1] Gilbert Bilezikian (1985). *Beyond the Sex Roles,* Baker Books

End of Chapter Questions
Chapter 2

1. What does the Bible say about women?
2. How did Gilbert Bilezikian, in his book "Beyond the Sex Roles," interpret God's creation design?
3. How would your vision for establishing a women's ministry coincide with the author's statement?
4. What purpose(s) and goal(s) would you select in preparing a statement for a particular outreach in your community?
5. What other function(s) would add to the organization model to make it more fulfilling for women's ministry?

Chapter 3 *Planning & Developing a Balanced Ministry*

What is your focus? What is your primary and secondary focus? There is a need to define where you are headed, before you begin to plan and implement ministry programs. Most women's ministry should be focused on two objectives – how to strengthen the Christian women and how to reach the non-Christian women who may never enter the door of a church.

Christian Women – You will be ministering to a whole spectrum of women who are in different levels of relationship with the Lord. Some have accepted the Lord as their Savior, however, some may not have a deep relationship with God, even though they may claim they do. Some move freely in spiritual gifts and others don't even understand what spiritual gifts are. You do not want to neglect Christian women, because they are a very important part of your women's ministry. Even these women need a new vision of their roles in the ministry.

Non-Christian Women – Who is the non-Christian woman? How will you reach her? These are questions your ministry should be asking. The non-Christian woman could be a co-worker, neighbor, hair designer – any woman from any walk of life. But whoever she is, she needs a personal relationship with the Lord. Often we are out of touch and clumsy in sharing the good news of Jesus Christ. Sometimes Christian women use clichés non-Christian women cannot understand.

It is so important that you plan and keep your meetings people-centered. Listed below are some key points regarding steps to keep your meetings people-centered.

1. An atmosphere of friendliness, concern, and caring for your attendees is the first step. The best way to implement this atmosphere is to decorate your meeting place according to the seasons of the year or a theme you are presenting. This will set the stage for a feeling of hospitality (you are welcome) and warmth for each individual that is attending. Welcome each individual with a special greeting, having a name card for them so each person can be addressed properly. Women want to be known as to who they are. It's a way to start a conversation by calling them by name. Names are good conversation starters.
2. Your audience needs to be a part of the meeting. Try to find ways to listen to and involve those attending your meeting. Realize that they represent different personalities, lifestyles,

gifting, and interests. As you welcome their involvement, you make them feel a sense of ownership in the group. This sends them a signal that you welcome different personalities, lifestyles, giftings, and interests. It will help ease everybody's natural insecurities to see that your group does not accept only certain stereotypes. It would be beneficial to your group to periodically take a poll on what areas of interest they would like to see presented in the future.

3. Try to use testimonies from women that speak profoundly about the power of the Lord in their lives. There is a special grace in real stories of encounters with difficult situations and how God was their helper in difficult times. He sustains us in our daily lives. Many women are won to the Lord through hearing testimonies that relate to their lives. Insights are shared that they are looking for, but have never been able to embrace because of their lack of knowledge, faith, prayer, and involvement with women who have fought the good fight and know how to touch the hem of our Master, Jesus. Even though some of their testimonies may seem simple, while other testimonies are profound, the important thing to remember is that a testimony takes courage, and leads toward self-acceptance.

In surveying successful and proven programs for women's ministries, I have found certain qualities that they must have in common. Listed below are some of the features or qualities that successful ministries share:

1. <u>Prayer</u> – An effective ministry will start with prayer. [1]
    a. Pray for the vision, plan, and purpose of the ministry.
    "Where there is no vision (no redemptive revelation of God), the people perish; but he who keeps the law (of God, which includes that of man) blessed (happy, fortunate, and enviable) is he." (Proverbs 29:18, Amplified); "Write the vision and make it plain on tablets," (Habakkuk 2:2 NKJ)
    b. Pray for workers to accomplish the vision such as helpers, altar workers, prayer warriors, staff members, praise and worship leader's, tape and sound workers, and cleanup crew.

"Having gifts (faculties, talents, qualities) that differ according to the grace given us, let us use them, (He whose gift is) prophecy, (let him prophesy) according to the proportion of his faith; (He whose gifts is) practical service, let him give himself to serving; He who exhorts (encourages), to his exhortation; he who contributes let him do it in simplicity and liberality; he who gives aid and superintends, with zeal and singleness of mind; he who does acts of mercy, with genuine cheerfulness and joyful eagerness" (Romans 12:6-8, Amplified)

c. Pray for finances to accomplish the vision.

"And they faithfully brought in the contributions, the tithes and the dedicated things" (II Chronicles 31:12, RS); "……and prove Me now by it, says the Lord of hosts, if I will not open the windows of heaven for you and pour you out a blessing, that there shall not be able room enough to receive it." (Malachi 3:10, Amplified)

d. Pray that the ministry gifts in the body will begin to function, and that all gifts will be working.

"Some of us have been given special ability as apostles; to others He has given the gift of being able to preach well; some have special ability in winning people to Christ; helping them to trust Him as their Savior; still others have a gift for caring for God's people as a shepherd does his sheep, leading and teaching them in the ways of God. (Ephesians 4:11-12, Living Bible)

e. Pray that the people will grow.

"That it might develop until we all attain oneness in the faith and in the comprehension of the (full and accurate) knowledge of the Son of God, that (we might arrive) at really mature manhood (the completeness of personality which is nothing less than the standard height of Christ's own perfection), the measure of the stature of the fullness of the Christ and the completeness found in Him." (Ephesians 4:13-14, Amplified)

f. Pray that the people will be faithful, dedicated, and committed.

"Moreover, it is (essentially) required of stewards that a man should be found faithful (proving himself worthy of trust). (I Corinthians 4:2, Amplified) "I will even betroth you to me in stability and in faithfulness, and you shall know

(recognize, be acquainted with, appreciate, give heed to, and cherish) the Lord." (Hosea 2:20, Amplified)

g. Pray that the people will be compassionate and loving.

"But if anyone has this world's goods, (resources for sustaining life) and sees his brother and fellow believer in need, yet closes his heart of compassion against him, how can the love of God live and remain in him?" (I John 17, Amplified); "Finally, all (of you) should be of one and the same mind (united in spirit), sympathizing (with one another), loving (each other) as brethren (of one household), compassionate and courteous (tenderhearted and humble). (I Peter 3:8, Amplified)

h. Pray that there will be unity and like-mindedness without division.

"Now may the God who gives the power of patient endurance (steadfastness) and Who supplies encouragement, grant you to live in such mutual harmony and such full sympathy with one anther, in accord with Christ Jesus. (Romans 15:5, Amplified); "Fill up and complete my joy by living in harmony and being of the same mind and one in purpose, having the same love, being in full accord and of one harmonious mind and intention." (Philippians 2:2, Amplified)

i. Pray for their eyes and ears to be opened, and bind spirits that hinder the women from receiving the fullness of the Word.

"I will rescue you from your own people and the Gentiles, I am sending you to open their eyes and turn from darkness to light, and from the power of Satan to God, so that they may receive forgiveness of sins and a place among those who are sanctified by faith in Me." (Acts 26:17-18, NIV)

j. Pray for the leadership as they minister, that they speak as the oracle of God, ministering with God's ability.

"Whoever speaks, (let him do it as one who utters) oracles of God; whoever renders service, (let him do it) as with the strength which God furnishes abundantly, so that in all things God may be glorified through Jesus Christ (the Messiah). To Him be the glory and dominion forever and ever (through endless ages)."

2. <u>Mentoring Disciples</u> – An effective minister knows how to mentor disciples. It's not enough that you have good attendance at your meetings, because these meetings should be a vehicle for reaching non-Christians as well as for fellowship, discipleship, and providing ministry to fellow Christians. Once women begin to attend, they will have varying interests, issues, and needs. These situations cannot be handled at each meeting, because your focus is presenting a Biblical topic or subject matter pertaining to life issues. Also, there isn't enough time to address the depth of these situations. Try to provide other opportunities for ministry, such as Bible studies, support groups, prayer counseling, or one-on-one mentoring, for those who need it, at another time.

There is a great need to nurture and encourage women in their walk with the Lord. When women's ministry creates an atmosphere open to innovation, they will equip the ministry to address, evaluate and receive feedback. This will help the ministry to not lose the cutting edge needed for women living in the twenty-first century. Today's interests, issues and needs are entirely different than they were in past history.

An innovative way to hold <u>Bible studies</u> may be to conduct them at a local place during lunch hours. With many women, there aren't enough minutes in the day to take care of all the family needs. Whether they are single, single-parent moms, or working moms, today's pressures are demanding. Perhaps an innovative <u>Support Group</u> would be effectively meeting before or right after work hours. <u>One-on-one mentoring</u> or <u>prayer counseling</u> could be done by phone at an appropriate time. Nurturing isn't limited to a particular time or situation. The hope is that it's occurring throughout the programs that have been established..

Let's look at these suggestions. As you participate in developing your ministry you will begin to see visually how effective brainstorming can help.

<u>Bible Study</u> – As your group begins to establish the time and place, the facilitator, and the curriculum, there needs to be some parameters set. Keep in mind that the time devoted to Bible study is the first priority. Bible study should not be longer than one hour, because most working women's lunch time is limited. If you pick a certain book of the Bible, character studies, or topical studies, try to limit the duration of the Bible study to not more than six weeks. It has been shown if the length of time is more than six weeks, the subject matter can become

redundant or overwhelming. It is better to select a beginning and an end to a topic, starting another topic each time. The teaching should include material for the unsaved, the new learner, and still have depth for the mature Christian. This approach might sound difficult, but as women become involved with each other, they help each other participate at their level. Remember it's all about relationship – getting involved and connected so that no one feels isolated or insecure. Another advantage of the shorter six-week duration is that there will be more women willing to teach for a shorter time, giving the attendees different viewpoints and insights to the studies. There should be breaks during the summer and holidays, if the attendees are in favor of taking the time off. For a more enhanced Bible study, the attendees should be instructed to read the material before each meeting. This will challenge the more mature Christians and help the new believers learn how to use the Bible. There are many excellent women's study books available in Christian bookstores for this purpose

Support Groups – As the group decides the appropriate time, place and facilitator, there also needs to be some parameters set for this group. As suggested, if the support group decides to meet one hour before or after work, there should be a fixed length for the duration of the support group. Then the group doesn't become the sole support entity for the women attending. Support groups can be a great help but also can be detracting to the full recovery of women becoming whole persons in Christ. It takes more than a group of women supporting one another. It takes involvement in the main meetings, developing relationship with the whole body, and training to develop their individual giftings. The support group can consist of single moms, parenting moms, single women, addictions, co-dependency, home schooling, etc. – whatever the need is in your area. When women see other women struggling with the same issues, they can be motivated to help each other and learn healthy skills. Be sure there is teaching on the facilitating of the group. The Bible tells us,

"My people are destroyed for lack of knowledge...." (Hosea 4:6, NKJ).

These support groups need a beginning and an end, so women can move on and be encouraged in their walk with the Lord. It's best to look at support groups as stepping-stones to encourage the believers along their road of reality, so that they don't take detours that lead to disillusionment or denial of situations in their lives.

One-on-One Mentoring – A very helpful group that can be established is to organize mentorship for women. Women who have never been taught about irrational beliefs (having faith in something that does not have reason or underlying principles and facts supporting it), instead of rational beliefs (according to reason, with underlying principles and facts) in their belief system need one-on-one mentoring in Biblical life principles. A woman dedicated to helping in this area can make a great difference in another woman's life by walking that extra mile to encourage her. Sometimes life circumstances can be so distracting that there is no way in their condition they will be able to participate in growing into a mature Christian. The women selected to oversee this part of the ministry and train other women will become a significant part of planning and developing a balance ministry.

<u>Prayer Counseling</u> – A prayer counselor is not a therapist. Prayer counselors can greatly assist those struggling to remove roadblocks along the journey of faith. This group of women is especially prepared to assist, willing to help others grow in the Lord. They are greatly used in the ministry of reconciliation.

"For all things are of God, who has reconciled us to Himself through Jesus Christ and has given us the ministry of reconciliation." (II Corinthians 5:18, NKJ)

An important aspect of prayer counseling is that it centers on a person, not a method. As the prayer counselor ministers God's Word, it frees the Holy Spirit to do His work in that person. It is done face to face by including gentle restoring to those who have erred. It includes healing of the soul from bitterness, unforgiveness, hurts, and ministering to the spirit when sin is blocking the relationship with God. Usually women come for divine counsel, not human counsel coming from you. The facilitator of this group should instruct the women who are going to be ministering in this area that there should be time for listening for direction from the Lord. Expect the gifts of the Spirit to be working during this time. Remember, the Lord is the real counselor,

"For to us a Child is born, to us a Son is given; and the government shall be upon His shoulder, and His name shall be called Wonderful Counselor, Mighty God, Everlasting Father (of Eternity), Prince of Peace." (Isaiah 9:6, Amplified).

Prayer counseling brings hope, and it involves communication with the one praying and the one seeking help. Prayer counseling is a tool to help keep your women's ministry a balanced ministry.

3. <u>Belief Statement</u> – In the interest of establishing a balanced ministry, every ministry should have their belief statement in writing, ready to distribute if attendees request the information. The following is a general statement prepared for developing your ministries' belief statement.

WHAT WE BELIEVE

- *We believe in one God – Father, Son, and Holy Spirit.*
- *We believe that the Lord Jesus Christ, the only begotten Son of God, was conceived of the Holy Spirit, born of the Virgin Mary; crucified; dead; buried and resurrected. He ascended into Heaven and is now seated at the right hand of God the Father and is true God and true man.*
- *We believe the Bible is the Word of God, fully inspired and written under the inspiration of the Holy Spirit and is our rule of faith and practice.*
- *We believe that all are born sinners; the Holy Spirit convicts of sin; the Lord Jesus Christ paid the price for sin by shedding His precious blood on the cross as the atonement for sin; those who refuse to accept His sacrifice for their sin are eternally lost; and those who repent of their sins and personally accept the Lord Jesus Christ as savior receive forgiveness of sin and life everlasting.*
- *We believe in he baptism in the Holy Spirit with the evidence of speaking in tongues as the Spirit of God gives utterance; that all of the gifts of the Holy Spirit are valid and operative today; and that the fruit of the Holy Spirit should be increasingly evident in a Christian's life.*
- *We believe that the redemptive work of the Lord Jesus Christ provides healing for our spirit, soul, and body.*
- *We believe that we should obey Jesus' command to preach the gospel to all the world.*
- *We believe in and look for the personal return of the Lord Jesus Christ.*

4. <u>Facilitating Meetings</u> – Before facilitating each meeting, there should be a pre-meeting of your leadership to decide all parts of the meeting to ensure it's in the manner you are proposing. Your goal is to make this a worthwhile meeting for your attendees to develop a better relationship with the Lord. It should be organized from beginning to end. Even though your group is flexible for change, when the Holy Spirit has a different agenda, the meeting should be

well organized, yet allow for a different direction from the Lord. This will help prevent distractions because of indecision or questions of duties that haven't been decided before the meeting begins. There should be an agenda for the leadership providing a track to run on, even if there are changes during the meeting. Handouts are not required for the attendees, but are sometimes helpful. Listed below are some guidelines as to how to start and maintain the ministry:

    a. Select a theme by accessing your resources through prayer. Different themes, inspired by the Holy Spirit, enhance the atmosphere, setting the direction of an inspiring meeting for your women. In order to keep the meetings balanced and interesting, your group should have a variety of speakers. It would be advised to use local and in-house speakers along with itinerant speakers to create interest, enhancing your chances of success.

    b. It is recommended that the women's ministry meeting use the same facility each time. It would be helpful if the meeting is weekly, bi-monthly or monthly and that it is kept on the same day/evening/week of the month. In order to not promote a certain church or denomination, it is sometimes better to consider a restaurant, hotel, club, youth center, etc. Meeting places should be clean and cheerful for a welcoming atmosphere.

    c. Expenses for each meeting should be evaluated and considered before each meeting. Expenses include honorariums for speakers, travel expenses, and any other incidental expenses required for the success of the meeting.

    d. Fellowship before the meeting is helpful so that the women may get acquainted. Refreshment before and after should be available to produce an atmosphere for fellowship. Having refreshments available helps set a stage for more intimate interaction between women.

    e. Nursery/child care could be optional - it depends on the audience your organization is intending to reach. Make sure you have qualified attendants to care for the children. This could enhance any organization's growth rate. Many women do not have or cannot afford a baby sitter. Quite often working mothers have been away from their children all day and would rather have them attend with them. Your staff could take turns serving by caring for the children.

    f. The meeting could include any combination of the following activities:

- Fellowship time

- Opening prayer, Announcements, Recognition of Visitors (Announcements- Other Times/Places for Bible Studies, Support Groups, Prayer Counseling, One-on-One Mentoring)
- Praise and Worship (half hour or less)
- Offering Time
- Special Music (if suggested)
- Speaker (one hour or less)
- Invitation for Salvation, Baptism of Holy Spirit, etc…
- Altar Ministry (Prayer Counseling to be scheduled for another time)
- Closing Prayer (Release women who need to leave)

In developing a fruitful, balanced ministry, it is beneficial to have a planning meeting each year. Have the weekly, bi-monthly, or monthly meetings, retreats, special events, etc. published by the first of each year with an available calendar to be given to all attendees and interested parties. Women like to be informed of details of the ministry they are attending and it helps the leadership remain accountable.

In the development of your ministry, record keeping is an important maintenance task. Some women's ministries have a yearly budget that is financed from their local church. Others may need to accept donations from those in attendance. Some may want to give tax deductible donations. If your ministry is going to be non-profit, the organization will be required to obtain the appropriate 501C3 status from the State and IRS as needed.

Another practical tool is to have "checkpoints" along the way to help your leadership keep in touch with your ever-changing audience and their needs. Success and failure has a way of teaching how valuable and essential it is for an effective-women's ministry to have an ongoing healthy program. Checkpoints that have been proven successful are ones that incorporate evaluation for which the foundation of your ministry is based and ones that continue to impact changes being made. Meetings for these "checkpoints" (feedback) should be scheduled periodically (three to four times a year), for more brainstorming and praying for the ongoing and future meetings. An overnight gathering may guarantee a more successful planning event. This gathering should be more people-centered than program centered. Some of the questions that should be addressed are as follows:

1. How can our group understand women's changing roles in today's world?
2. Whom are we actually reaching and how can we expand our audience?
3. What are their greatest needs and are we fulfilling them?
4. What are our strengths/weaknesses and how can we improve them?
5. What changes do we need to make and how can we implement them?

These questions and many more can stimulate the group toward innovative ideas to improve the ministry.

Another consideration would be to have advisors who could critique all areas of the ministry. If they were available to attend some of your events and leadership meetings, they could provide valuable feedback. Accountability to others is a saving grace. By not becoming a "clique," which in time stunts the growth of any organization, you become more effective for God.

Hopefully, these comments have been helpful in planning and developing a balanced ministry.

References:

[1] John Delgado, Ph.D. (2000). *Prayer Training Manual.* John Delgado Ministries, West Palm Beach, FL

End of Chapter Questions
Chapter 3

1. What are the two objectives women's ministry should focus on?
2. What are the keys to keeping your meetings people-centered?
3. In planning and implementing a ministry, what are the four features and qualities in developing a successful ministry?

    a. _____

    b. _____

    c. _____

    d. _____

4. From the previous question write a short paragraph evaluating each of your answers.
5. What are some "checkpoints" a ministry should have? List some others that you would implement in a ministry.

Chapter 4 *Ways to Implement a Ministry*

There are many ways to implement a ministry, but first, let us look at some of the challenges to implementation:

1. <u>Creating an interest in the ministry</u>. There may be many women's ministries in a given city or town. The first thing necessary for a ministry to be implemented is to create an interest in what yours has to offer. If the Lord has laid on your heart a ministry in your church or locality, He will give you the plan. If God isn't the author and director of the plan, it is destined to failure. In Chapter one we emphasized the need to start with a questionnaire. The questionnaire will facilitate the interests of your audience. Once you learn the heartbeat of the women you will minister to and establish the goals for the beginning of your ministry as described in the previous chapters, you are on your way to facilitating your ministry. First you must have genuine interest and excitement.

2. <u>Find ways to communicate</u> the importance and opportunities your ministry has to offer to women. This will generally help the women to have open eyes and ears to what part they will participate in. Generally, women desire to be a part of a group that is developing new and exciting ideas to fill a need. They want to be on the ground floor of implementation.

3. <u>Time and energy</u> in today's culture is one of the most challenging aspects of ministry development, due in part to the fast pace of life. Determining the right time and place to facilitate the ministry, coupled with adjustments for women's busy lives, will take some planning.

Let's look at some creative ways to implement women's ministries, to overcome some of the challenges just mentioned.

<u>Publicity and Promotion</u>
- Mail outs – Using mailouts to promote your women's ministry requires the development of a computer database. If your ministry is part of your local church, your computer database will begin with the church membership list. The church list will give a head start in developing your potential list of attendees. Using directories of local churches, faith-based ministries (such as recovery homes, shelters, outreaches, etc.), local

merchants, and community activities in your area will also help develop a computer base for your mailout. Once you have your ministry underway, a monthly newsletter with your activities, available opportunities, and women's testimonies will help stimulate interest from those being reached by your mailings. To keep the postage at a minimum, postcards are another vehicle your ministry can use to get the information out to your community.

- Web-site – Many different organizations and businesses use a web-site. Designing your web-site can be quite a challenge in reaching the audience you are trying to attract. Women are attracted to other women that are concerned not only for their spiritual life, but also about local, family, or school issues. Remember, a Christian women's ministry is not only reaching out to the believer, but also to the non-believer. If possible, present the ministry as an inter-denominational outreach with the purpose of women growing and developing in their God-given purpose and potential. Advertise and promote a meeting occasionally in a community center building, where women can come and check out what your ministry is all about.

- E-Mail – E-mail promotion can be very helpful. On your web-site and mail out, be sure you include your ministry E-mail address. The success of your E-mail communication will depend on the ministry having a facilitator to evaluate and respond to each E-mail in a timely manner. People that use this type of communication want to have a response to their messages. It is a great way to publicize your ministry. Adding Bible verses and small devotions may perk interest in your ministry as you present spiritual points from the Bible. Taking prayer requests from your readers makes it more personal and caring. Promote the fact that your ministry cares about all areas of their life and desires to help in daily concerns.

- Special Events – Reaching out through special events will draw women in a non-threatening way who might not otherwise participate in Church or Christian-associated activities. The group you're targeting to reach will determine the type of event you will promote.

Events such as an English Tea advertised at a local restaurant targeted as a social gathering of your community with a well-known speaker speaking on women's issues, promoting the importance of women getting together to fellowship, keeping in touch to discuss important issues they have in their everyday lives.

A fashion show with the latest fashions from retail stores in your area is always a great interest to women. You would be surprised how local, well-known, retail stores are anxious for the community to have their merchandise displayed. Using creative ideas, you could choose some women from the Bible to demonstrate (if they were alive today), an outfit they would probably have worn. Coupled with a small devotion on women of the Bible, this enhances your special event, bridging yesterday into today.

A Christmas party sharing the birth of Jesus is another evangelistic event, which will offer a way of reaching out in your community. A clubhouse, a gated community center, or a home, for a more intimate environment, are ideal for places to hold this type of fellowship. Presenting Jesus at this time of the year is very accepting to believers or women seeking to believe. Hearts are more open during the holiday season.

Keep these events fun and interesting to your audience. Women caring for other women, their families, and related issues will attract a large group. Having resources available in your community for the group promotes your interest in their needs. The cost of these different events could be covered by ticket sales or by some of your women sponsoring a person, or a love gift. Be sure, if you decide to implement a special event, that you have a committee established to complete all the tasks needed to make this event successful.

- Advertising – In most communities there are community papers that you can advertise in. Some are free and others can be solicited for a minimal cost. You would be surprised at the number of people in any community that read these local papers. Of course, you can advertise in your city paper monthly as an investment into your ministry. There may be a Christian newspaper that you can advertise in. However, to reach the non-Christian and the unreached, they seldom read a Christian paper. They may genuinely be searching for something, but are not sure what it is they are looking for. If you provide a subject of interest or some information important to them, they will respond. That is why it is important to target all people in all walks of life. If your ministry has a food bank, clothing or thrift store, those needing such devices will find you if you advertise where they are likely to see you. Many people gravitate to an organization that has been there for them in times of physical and emotional need. When they had these needs taken care of and trust is established between them and the ministry, they will feel that the ministry can help them in their spiritual needs as well. There are many testimonies regarding the impact a ministry has on individuals, simply because they answered a basic need at a time when there were no other resources available to them.

<u>Evangelism</u>

- Personal Evangelism - Personal evangelism should be the concern of every believer. Personal evangelism is a personal touch on a woman's life at a strategic time when all else seems impossible. Evangelism occurs when we get to know a circle of people that the Lord has set up for a divine appointment for an encounter with you and Christ. This includes women like your hairdresser, cashiers at a department or grocery store, the nurse or doctor's office, fellow workers at your place of work, neighbors, people you meet while traveling, encounters at local amusement parks – these are all candidates for divine appointments. You never know when, in a split second, the Lord could put you in an individual's life when they need to hear encouragement in a time of need. You have available to you, at that moment in time, the answer that can help this individual.

It is wise for your ministry to print cards to be made available to pass out with the times and place of your meeting. These cards could mention other activities available, such as: Bible studies, support groups, etc. Further, your cards should give your name and phone number. When presented, you can then talk about how your women's ministry has helped you and give her a brief testimony (if there is time). You can then share how women's ministry can provide physical, emotional and spiritual contact with other women. This can be a bridge to someone, assisting them on their journey to become whole in their walk with Christ. Sometimes, starting to attend church can be too much for them at first (not knowing anyone), but a meeting with women is less threatening. Personal evangelism is very close to the Lord's heart. He said,

"All authority has been given to Me in heaven and on earth. Go therefore and make disciples of all the nations…" (Matthew 28:18-19)

When we consider personal evangelism, many think of large groups such as stadium crusades, etc. We have an evangelistic field in our own backyard. When a wheat field is being harvested, we only harvest one shock of wheat at a time (a shock of wheat representing our realm of influence). Each one of us could win the world if we did so one by one. If we get caught up looking at the whole wheat field we will miss the shocks right at our feet.

- Telephone Evangelism - Calling is an important part of advertising your ministry. Local calls are free, but it does take time to use this kind of communication. If your ministry is based out of your church, you will already have a telephone directory to use. If your women's ministry is focused in your community with a specific group of women you are targeting, a telephone directory can be more challenging. Take your local phone book and begin to call, asking for the lady of the house. Let it be known that you are not advertising a product or a service, just calling to give information on upcoming events in your community. Be sure you select women who are cheerful (not pushy), who have an evangelistic interest in calling. Some women are very shy about calling, because most of them feel they are intruding. Usually those women are better at calling after they have attended meetings encouraging new contacts, making them feel important to your group. Telephoning at the right time is also important. Be sure to ask the person you are calling, if this is a good time or should they call later. Women are usually cordial when you sound sincere in what you are calling about. They welcome someone taking the time to be interested in their lives.

    Another great tool is having information available to your caller in regards to promises in the Bible, in case the women you are calling begin to ask questions. Be prepared to pray with the women if this is applicable. As the women you are calling raise the different questions, write them down. Knowing these questions can help to equip the callers to be more effective while gaining insight into the community you serve.

- Canvassing - When organizing your outreach, it would be helpful to have a map of the location you are canvassing. This is not only for a better interpretation of the area, but also for documentation of places in that area you have already canvassed. Praying over the map and praying for the people in that location is a valuable way to start. It is good to educate your women on the importance of going door-to-door for a personal touch. Many women enjoy canvassing in their neighborhoods, communities, and areas of interest. It is important to have material available to give out to those you meet and talk to. We mentioned before having business cards with your ministry's information on it, but also have available a brochure telling about your ministry.

In Appendix I we have a sample brochure for you to consider for your ministry. A brochure should consist of your mission statement, goals, and what your ministry is about. Placing the information in the visitor's hand will help them to have something to remember you by in the future. Bookmarks, or a pen with your ministry's information on it, are other ways to keep your ministry in front of the women you are reaching out to.

Be courteous to the person who comes to the door. If they are busy at the time, ask them if you could leave the information before you depart. Be prepared to minister to the people during your visit. You never know what is happening in their homes. This could be one of those divine appointments God has ordained for you. The Bible tells us He sent them out two by two. I would advise you to have no more than two standing at the door (others could stand on the sidewalk waiting), because it could make the home-owners feel intimated. Professionalism and confidence in the Lord's work always helps you when you are canvassing different locations.

Implementing a ministry is an on-going task which can also be enhanced by a bi-weekly or monthly newsletter. The newsletter could contain announcements of up-coming events, an occasional testimony, and information on your mission, goals and plans for accomplishing your ministry. The newsletter could also include details on ministry opportunities and encourage the women to participate. Continually implementing your ministry will always be a challenge. In order to keep the energy and vitality up in your ministry, innovative ideas should be continually sought after. Finally, the advertising thrust of any women's ministry should also utilize church marquees, community bulletin boards, and public service announcements whenever possible.

End of Chapter Questions
Chapter 4

1. What are the key challenging issues to keep in mind when implementing a women's ministry?

2. List some publicity and promotions methods used in this chapter to implement an on-going successful women's ministry.

3. Create a special Christian event and design it for a group of women in a community that could be targeted toward women's interests.

4. List some evangelistic methods that could be used to reach believers and non-believers to be interested in participating in a women's ministry.

5. What is your interpretation of the importance of having a plan to implement an effective group of women?

Part 2

TRAINING, PREPARATION, & MOTIVATION

"Now there are distinctive varieties and distributions of endowments (gifts, extraordinary powers, distinguishing certain Christians, due to the power of divine grace operating in their souls by the Holy Spirit) and they vary, but the (Holy) Spirit remains the same. And there are distinctive varieties of service and ministration, but it is the same Lord (Who is served)….But to each one is given the manifestation of the (Holy) Spirit (the evidence, the spiritual illumination of the Spirit) for good and profit."

(I Corinthians 12:4-5, 7, Amplified)

PART 2: Training, Preparation, & Motivation

It is important to provide training for your potential leaders and on-going leaders in order to keep your ministry moving successfully and being on the cutting edge of quality ministry. There is a need to have, if possible, what has been coined "Ministers in Training" (MIT). Deciding to have certain training classes protects your ministry from having wounded soldiers. Our armed forces, companies, most work places, athletics, managerial positions, etc., all over the country have periodical training for their leaders and others in appointed positions. Without training it is hard for anyone to grasp and catch the motivation of your mission and goal as your ministry grows. If some of your MITs want to pursue Bible college classes, this would be very helpful. But in the absence of personal, on the spot oversight, many will not develop their God-given gifts. It is only through training and being used in practical ministry that leaders are developed. That is why most growing churches today have a training campus for developing leaders. In the New Testament when the need was the greatest this was God's plan and today it is working also.

"You therefore, my son, be strong in the grace that is in Christ Jesus. And the things that you have heard from me among many witnesses, commit these to faithful men who will be able to teach others also. You therefore must endure hardship as a good soldier of Jesus Christ. No one engaged in warfare entangles himself with the affairs of this life, that he may please him who enlisted him as a soldier. And also if anyone competes in athletics, he is not crowned unless he competes according to the rules." (II Timothy 2:1-5)

Chapter 5 *Building Your Leadership Team*

There is no particular formula for building your leadership team. Many books have been written on leadership, and each endeavors to instruct your ministry how to develop good leadership. In building your leadership team there are certain key elements to be considered.

A true leader is first a disciple. As a disciple, he/she must:[1]

- *Be willing to serve (Mark 10:35-45*
- *Be willing to learn and have a teachable spirit (Matthew 16:22-23)*
- *Be submissive to legitimate authority (Hebrews 13:17)*
- *Be willing to share their faith (I John 1:1-13*
- *Exhibit humility (Philippians 2:3-4)*
- *Be forgiving (Matthew 18:21)*
- *Be persistent and courageous (Ephesians 6:10-18)*
- *Be trustworthy and responsible (I Corinthians 4:2)*
- *Use time wisely (Ephesians 5:15-17)*
- *Be quick to obey God (Luke 5:4-9)*
- *Have faith in God, not just faith in faith (Mark 11:20-22)*

The first and foremost quality of a leader is the willingness to serve. If you select a leader that doesn't have that quality, most likely they will assert their own agenda. When Jesus was teaching His disciples, He declared to His disciples that He must go to Jerusalem and suffer many things at the hands of the elders, and the Chief priest and scribes, and that He would be killed, and on the third day be risen from the dead. When Peter heard this, he took the Lord aside privately and began to correct Him saying:

"...God forbid, Lord! This must never happen to you! But Jesus turned away from Peter and said to him, Get behind Me, Satan! You are in My way (an offense and hindrance and a snare to Me); for you are minding what partakes, not of the nature and quality of God, but of men" (Matthews 16:23 Amplified)

Jesus went on to tell them that if they desired to be His disciples, they would have to deny themselves and their interests. They would have to be willing to learn to have a teachable spirit.

"....whoever desires to be great among you must be your servant. And whoever wishes to be most important and first in rank among you must be slave of all. For even the Son of Man came not to have service rendered to Him, but to serve, and to give His life as a ransom for many." (Mark 10:43-45, Amplified)

Jesus is our model of ministry; He showed us how to prepare leaders. Jesus had men and women in His broad circle of followers. They were all His disciples ministering in different capacities. He modeled leadership with a balance of servanthood and authority.

Te develop women leaders, we start by asking women to be involved. This begins the leadership development process. In your women's ministry don't be overwhelmed by the need to fill every position. In a previous chapter we described the many jobs needed for different areas for ministry. To begin to fill leadership positions with qualified candidates, women need to apply. Following is an application (see page 63 for a sample) for the women to fill out for your committee to select your core ministry group. This is a most important project for your initial group to accomplish; the development of an informative application for selecting your key leaders. You could also have the applicants submit a resume of all their involvements in other ministries they have been associated with. This would be an informative tool in selecting potential leaders.

In selecting, building, and developing your leadership team there are many facets to consider. Listed below are some insights to consider.

<u>Characteristics of a Leader</u>
- a. <u>The definition of character</u> – As defined by Webster's Dictionary, character is a distinctive trait, quality, or attribute; characteristics. The pattern of behavior or personality found in an individual or group; moral constitution. Moral strength; self-discipline, fortitude, good reputation.
- b. <u>Character qualification of a leader</u> – It can be summed up by positive qualities in a person's life by their actions, attitudes, thoughts, values, and motivations. In a person's inner life, character traits can be reflected by sinful nature or divine nature, depending on negative or positive qualities in their lives.

APPLICATION

Name for Women's Ministry

Applicant Name: _____

Address: _____

City: _____ State: _____ Zip _____

Phone: _____ E-mail: _____

GENERAL INFORATION

( ) Single   ( ) Married   ( ) Divorced   ( ) Widowed

Husband's Name (if married) _____

Are you an active member in your Church? ( ) Yes   ( ) No

Do you serve in a Church position? ( ) Yes   ( ) No

Position: _____ How long? _____

Name & Address of Church you Attend: _____

_____

Pastor's Name _____ Pastor's Phone No. _____

Briefly tell how and when you received Jesus as your Savior:

_____

_____

What Christian work are you doing at the present time:

_____

_____

Are you a Leader in any other groups? ( ) Yes   ( ) No

(If so, name): _____

List two references, their addresses, and phone numbers::

_____

_____

_____

_____

Applicant's Signature _____ Date _____

Figure 5.0 Application (Sample)

Character Development of a Leader

    a. <u>The process of Developing Leadership</u> - II Peter 1:1-11 in the Amplified Bible describes the growth methods in developing Christian traits for leadership. *"Simon Peter, a servant and apostle (special messenger) of Jesus Christ, to those who have received (obtained an equal privilege of) like precious faith with ourselves in and through the righteousness of our God and Savior Jesus Christ. May grace (God's favor), and peace (which is perfect, well-being, all necessary good, all spiritual prosperity, and freedom from fears and agitating passions and moral conflicts) be multiplied to you in (the full, personal, precise, and correct) knowledge of God and of Jesus our Lord. For His divine power has bestowed upon us all things that (are requisite and suited) to life and godliness, through the (full, personal) knowledge of Him, Who called us by and to His own glory and excellence (virtue). By means of these He has bestowed on us His precious and exceedingly great promises, so that through them you may escape (by flight) from the moral decay (rottenness and corruption) that is in the world because of covetousness (lust and greed), and become sharers (partakers) of the divine nature. For this very reason adding your <u>diligence</u> (to the divine promises), employ every effort in exercising your <u>faith</u> to develop virtue (excellence, resolution, Christian energy), and in (exercising) <u>virtue</u> (develop), knowledge (intelligence), and in (exercising) <u>knowledge</u> (develop) self-control, and in (exercising) <u>self-control</u>, and in (develop) steadfastness (patience, endurance), and in (exercising) <u>steadfastness</u> (develop) godliness (piety). And in (exercising) <u>godliness</u> (develop) brotherly affection, and in (exercising) <u>brotherly affection</u> (develop) Christian <u>love</u>. For as these qualities are yours and increasingly abound in you, they will keep (you) from being idle or unfruitful unto the (full personal) knowledge our Lord Jesus Christ (the Messiah, the Anointed One). For whoever lacks these qualities is blind, (spiritually) shortsighted, seeing only what is near to him, and has become oblivious (to the fact) that he was cleansed from his old sins. Because of this, brethren, be all the more solicitous and eager to make sure (to ratify, to strengthen, to make steadfast) your calling and election for if you do this, you will never stumble or fall. Thus there will be richly* *and abundantly provided for you entry into the eternal kingdom of our Lord and savior Jesus Christ!*

Let's review some of these key progressive qualities:

1. <u>Diligence</u> - The quality of being diligent; constant, careful effort; perseverance (*added to your faith*).
2. <u>Faith</u> – The unquestioning belief that does not require proof or evidence (*added to your virtue*).
3. <u>Virtue</u> – General moral excellence; right action and thinking; goodness or morality (*added to knowledge*).
4. <u>Knowledge</u> – The act or fact, or state of knowing, acquaintance with facts; range of information (*added to temperance*).
5. <u>Temperance</u> – The state or quality of being temperate; self-restraint in conduct; moderation in indulging the appetites (*added to patience*).
6. <u>Patience</u> – The act of bearing or endearing trouble, pain, anguish without complaining or losing self-control, forbearing, tolerance (*added to Godliness*).
7. <u>Godliness</u> – Devoted to God and acknowledging the existence of God in devotion to Him (*added to brotherly kindness*).
8. <u>Brotherly Kindness</u> - Having traits considered typical to a brother; friendly, kind, helpful and caring (*added to love*).
9. <u>Love</u> – A deep and tender feeling of affection or attachment or devotion to persons and God.

This surely describes the process of developing character in a Christian life.

b. <u>The Potential Leader's Responsibility:</u>

The leader as a believer has responsibilities too. As a believer he/she must apply God's divine nature through the power of the Holy Spirit. God has given believers all the necessary tools to implement His divine character in their daily life with the Lord. These are principles to look for in potential leaders. Do they spend time daily in the word and do they know how to apply those principles to live an overcoming life daily? Are they accountable to a spiritual leader (pastor, overseer, believing husband)? Do they walk in the authority of Jesus Christ in all areas of their lives?

"And all of us, as with unveiled face, (because we) continued to behold (in the Word of God) as in a mirror the glory of the Lord, are constantly being transformed into His very image in ever increasing splendor and from one degree of glory to another; (for this comes) from the Lord (Who is) the Spirit." (Amplified)

<u>Major Character Areas for Christian leaders</u>

The Christian leader today must develop their character in these eight major areas of life: [2]

1. Spiritual life – A leader's relationship with the Lord is built upon godly character as well as a depth of intimacy through God's Word and prayer.

2. Personal life – The habits, lifestyle and patterns which a leader develops will have a great influence upon the ministry she has received from the Lord.

3. Home life – A leader's personal family life will form the basis for her ministry to the family of God. A leader must first have her own house in order. This is based upon her character, for without character she will have no successful family life.

4. Social life – A leader's friendships reflect her character. A leader must develop character to have successful social relationships. Loyalty and acceptance are two great factors required in friendships. If a woman has character, she will have the needed elements for a normal and healthy social life.

5. Educational life – Education by itself is not enough to build good character. But if character is developed through the disciplines of life, education can be a powerful force in the life of a leader. A good character enables a leader to receive a good education in and out of the classroom.

6. Ministerial life – Character is the root of all that a governmental ministry does. Ministry function is, in itself, a manifestation of a leader's character. What she is will come out in what she does in her ministry. I Timothy 3 and Titus 1 list character qualifications as the basis for a leader's ministerial life.

7. Marital life – A leader's marital life will succeed only as she has a mature and developed character. A woman without a developed character brings her deficiencies

into the home with her. A leader's married life will blossom only if her character is cultivated: otherwise, she will never be able to meet the needs of her husband.

8. Financial life – Jesus Christ said that if a man/woman did not know how to take care of money, that God would not commit to him/her the true spiritual riches of the kingdom. A leader's frugality, wisdom, true desires, values, self-esteem, and ability to give are all demonstrated by how they use the money that they have (though not necessarily by how much money they earn).

These are some great principles for a Christian leader to develop in order to achieve God's goal for them. Building your leadership team takes much preparation and prayer. Many organizations emphasize the gifts or charisma of the leader, far above their character development. The imbalance can cause many problems. There needs to be a balance between gifts and character.

References:

[1] Stan DeKoven, Ph.D.(1994. *Leadership and Vision.* Vision Publishing, Ramona, CA.

[2] Frank Damazio (1998). *The Making of a Leader* . City Bible Publishing

End of Chapter Questions
Chapter 5

1. What is the first and most important quality a leader must have and why is this quality so important in building a leadership team?
2. In preparing an application for a ministry, what would your requirements contain?
3. What qualifications of a potential leader do you find is necessary?
4. In the process of developing leaders, in a paragraph, describe what you feel is most important.
5. In the description of major character areas of Christian leaders, how would you describe how important a leader's character is in her personal life?

Chapter 6 *Tools to Help Women Develop Their Call & Gifts*

God gives spiritual gifts and power to each person through His Spirit. These gifts accomplish His will in believers which allows them to minister to one another in the Body of Christ. One of the first steps for a believer in discovering God's plan for their life is to discover their spiritual gifts.

I. <u>Teaching Women How To Find Their Spiritual Gifts</u>
   A. Brief History Review - Indwelling of Holy Spirit for Believers
   - The Holy Spirit moved powerfully in the Early Church. (Book of Acts)
   - Interest in the Holy Spirit and His gifts waned in early Church History. (after the Book of Acts)
   - Renewed interest in the Holy Spirit emerged again in the early 1900s. Charles Parham of Topeka Kansas laid hands on Agnes Ozman who began speaking in tongues. The Azusa Street revival (LA) began in 1906 under William Seymour.
   - Present day Pentecostal Churches were formed such as Assemblies of God, Pentecostal Holiness, Church of God in Christ, Church of the Foursquare Gospel, Church of God, etc.
   - Second Phase began after WWII
   - Renewed interest in the work of the Holy Spirit and spiritual gifts emerged in the 70s

   B. How to discover your Spiritual Gifts
      1. Discover Spiritual Gifts by surrendering to God

         (Romans 12:1, NKJ) – "I beseech you therefore, brethren by the mercies of God, that you present your bodies a living sacrifice, holy, acceptable to God, which is your reasonable service."

         Make a decision to commit and submit to God's will by making yourself available to spending time in His presence.
      2. Discover your Spiritual Gifts by being transformed by God

         (Romans 12:2, NKJ) – "And do not be conformed to this world, but be transformed by the renewing of your mind, that you may prove what is that good and acceptable and perfect will of God."

God's way of thinking is revealed in His Word. The way to renew your mind is by studying the Word of God. By faith we can see who God is and have Him reveal who we are in our relationship with Him.

3. Discover Spiritual Gifts by being responsible.

(Romans 12:3-5, Amplified) "For by the grace (unmerited favor of God) given to me I warn everyone among you not to estimate and think of himself more highly than he ought (not to have an exaggerated opinion of his own importance), but to rate his ability with sober judgment, each according to the degree of faith apportioned by God to him. For as in one physical body we have many parts (organs, members) and all of these parts do not have the same function or use. So we, numerous as we are, are one body in Christ (the Messiah) and individually we are parts one of another (mutually dependent on one another)."

The lost need the simple gospel and as leaders there is a need to be "other conscious." The body of Christ has many needs and it takes all parts of the body and their giftings to fulfill His commission in our lives.

4. Discover Spiritual Gifts just as you discover your natural gifts.

As a leader, or when mentoring women in discovering their spiritual gifts, one of the best ways to discover them is just like you discovered your natural gifts. Experiment with as many gifts as you can. Be available and get to know gifted people. Seek out and talk to women who have discovered and developed their spiritual gift by using them. Evaluate your effectiveness in experimenting in the different gifts. If you experiment with a gift and find what the gift is supposed to do doesn't happen, you probably have discovered that it is not one of the gifts God has given you. If the true gift is in operation, what is intended to happen will happen. In experimenting in the gifts, expect confirmation from the Body of Christ. Conformation is important, because it produces a system of accountability in the use of gifts. God's plan is for us to discover our spiritual gift and use them to edify the Body of Christ.

C. Facts about Spiritual Gifts – Listed below are three main categories:

- God's Gifts to the Church – <u>Motivational Gifts</u> *(Romans 12:6-8)*

- *Prophecy, Serving, Teaching, Exhortation, Giving, Ruling/Organization, Mercy*
♦ Son's Gifts to the Church – <u>Ministry Gifts</u> (*Ephesians 4:11*)
  - *Apostle, Prophet, Evangelist, Pastor, Teacher*
♦ Holy Spirit's Gifts to the Church – <u>Charismatic Gifts</u> (*I Corinthians 12:7-11*)
  - *Gifts of Revelation, Gifts of Power, Gifts of Utterance*

1. God's Gifts to the Church (<u>Motivational Gifts</u>) - A Motivational Gift is an inner motivation in your spirit (not personality) which was imparted to you at your natural birth. The gift motivates you to meet certain needs and it moves you from within, you don't move it. It's a portion of the heart of Christ.

   (Romans 12:6-8, Amplified) "Having gifts (faculties, talents, qualities) that differ according to the grace given us, let us use them; (He whose gift is) prophecy, (let him prophesy) according to the proportion of his faith; (He whose gift is) practical service, let him give himself to serving; he who teaches, to his teaching; He who exhorts (encourages), to his exhortation; he who contributes, let him do it in simplicity and liberality; he who gives (giving) aid and superintends with zeal and singleness of mind; he who does acts of mercy, with genuine cheerfulness and joyful eagerness." [1]

   a. <u>Prophecy</u> – A woman that has the gift of prophecy will have insight or an intuitive sense about people and situations as they really are before God. They passionately defend God's standards and have discernment about what happens to people who compromise God's standards.

   Traits listed:
   ♦ Perceives character and hidden motives, good or bad
   ♦ Exposes them (verbally, dramatic, direct).
   ♦ Uncompromising when confronting and can be fearful afterward.
   ♦ Passionate about honoring God and His will.
   ♦ Desires to produce repentance and brokenness and touches the conscience.

   <u>*Biblical Woman Example*</u> *– Deborah (Judges 4:1-24)*

b. <u>Serving</u> – A woman that has the gift of serving meets the practical needs of others in love. She demonstrates love in deeds and not words. This person likes to work behind the scenes. She has an alertness to detect and meet practical needs, before anyone else notices.

Traits listed:

- Perceives and satisfies needs.
- Develops and uses skills.
- Move quickly and with quality work.
- Hard to say "no."
- Needs appreciation, because she sees it as the Lord's approval.
- Works alone and is very friendly. Sees people hindered by lack of ability, and moves in.

<u>Biblical Woman Example</u> – Phoebe (Romans 16:2)

c. <u>Teaching</u> – A woman that has the gift of teaching has the ability to communicate information pertinent to the subject material. That will minister to the body of Christ in such a way that others will learn the fullness of God's Word and its application to live the abundant life in Christ.

- Desire to intensively study the Word in detail from beginning to end.
- Organizes truth into doctrine (not dogma).
- Wants to be established and establish others doctrinally.
- Receives and ministers revelation in scriptures.
- Imparts understanding.
- Prefers scriptural illustrations.
- Sees the need and harm of ignorance of scriptural knowledge.

<u>Biblical Woman's Example</u> – Lois and Eunice (II Timothy 1:5 & II Timothy 3:14-15).

d. <u>Exhortation</u> – A woman that has the gift of exhortation, with the ability to minister encouragement to the body of Christ. She desires to see believers live an overcoming life in Christ using practical Biblical principles. Many with this gift have words of comfort and counsel in ways that can bring healing to the body of Christ.

- Stimulates the faith of others to walk in Christian success and victory.
- Enjoys the abundant life and inspires others to it.
- Is enthusiastic, creative, inspirational and conversational and sees value of tribulation and affliction.
- Perceives discouragement and gives steps to follow.
- Very accepting, encouraging, challenging to action.
- Adventurous and bold.

Biblical Woman Example – Esther (Book of Esther)

e. Giving – A woman that has the gift of giving, with the ability to give, donate, or bestow their material to the work of the Lord with a willingness to share freely with cheerfulness.

- Perceives material lack.
- Spiritual need to give, contribute, share, entrust, to further the ministry.
- Financially wise and prudent.
- Inspires others to give and gives quality gifts.
- Strong trust in God's provision.
- Gives quietly, is frugal and not gullible.

Biblical Woman Example - Lydia (Acts 16:14-15)

f. Ruling/ Organization – A woman that has the gift of ruling/organizations has the ability to understand clearly the immediate and long-range goals of facilitating a task or project. She is an organizer and loves new challenges to devise and execute effective plans for the accomplishment of those goals.

- Desires to coordinate people and resources to complete tasks together.
- Promotes teamwork to achieve common goals.
- Very conscious of available resources and of peoples' skills and giftings.
- Resistant to negative criticism.

- Decisive and moves on to new goals quickly.
- Visionary with broad perspective and dislikes routine tasks.
- Can overlook character flaws and has a high-powered personality (daring).

<u>*Biblical Woman Example*</u> – *Martha (Luke 10:38-42)*

g. <u>Mercy</u> – A woman that has the gift of mercy has the ability to feel real empathy and compassion for individuals (both Christian and no Christian) who suffer mental, physical, or emotional problems, and to translate that compassion into deeds which reflect Christ's love and relieve or reduce the suffering.

- Fulfilled in showing mercy (good listener and gentle).
- Has outward display of compassion, not just inward feeling.
- Reaches out to emotionally-troubled, distressed, wounded persons.
- Ability to sense emotional temperature of a crowd (discerning).
- Motivated to minister healing of hurts.
- Sensitivity to hurtful words and actions (seeks harmony).
- Trusting and defender of good causes.

<u>*Biblical Woman Example*</u> – *Naomi (Book of Ruth)*

NOTE: See Appendix 2 for a Motivational Gifts Test

2. Son's Gifts to the Church (<u>Ministry Gifts</u>) – The Ministry Gifts were given to the church so the body of Christ could function properly and reach maturity. They are called the five-fold ministry. The five-fold ministry (apostle, prophet, evangelist, pastor and teacher) is to prepare the members to be able ministers of the Gospel. Jesus fulfilled all five of these ministry gifts.

(Ephesians 4:11, Amplified) "And His gifts were (varied. He Himself appointed and gave men to us) some to be apostles (special messengers), some prophets (inspired preachers and expounders), some evangelists (preachers of the Gospel, traveling missionaries, some pastors (shepherds of His flock) and teachers."

a. Apostle - The Greek word, *apostolos*, translated apostle, means one sent forth, a sent one. An apostle has the ability to exercise leadership over a number of churches with an authority in spiritual matters recognized by those churches.

b. Prophet – The Greek word, *prohetes*, translated prophet, means to foretell events, divine, to speak under inspiration. A prophet has the ability to declare the Word of God with anointing, convicting the hearers, so they know that it is the Word of God and they are compelled to do something about it.

c. Evangelist – The Greek word, *euangelistes*, translated evangelist, means a messenger of good tidings. An evangelist has the ability to bring the gospel to unbelievers so that men and women accept Jesus, becoming disciples and part of the Body of Christ.

d. Pastor – The Greek word, *poinen*, translated pastor, means shepherd, one who tends herds or flocks, guides as well as feeds the flock, overseer. A pastor has the ability to maintain a long-term personal responsibility for the well-being of a group of believers spiritually.

e. Teacher – The Greek word, *didaskalos* translated teacher, means an instructor. A teacher has the ability to communicate information pertinent to a biblical study that will minister to the body of Christ in a way that others will learn.

Each part of the five-fold ministry was designed to have the same goal. They are:

- Equip and train God's people for works of service.
- Disciple and build the body of Christ.
- Teach the principles of the Son of God.

The gifts Jesus gave to the church were so the body could function properly.

NOTE: The five-fold ministry gifts are more fully explained in C. Peter Wagner's book, *"Your Spiritual Gifts Can Help Your Church Grow."* If your women's group desires gift testing in this area, contact their ministry for that information. (*Gospel Light Publishers 1-800-4-GOSPEL)*

3. Holy Spirit Gifts to the Church (Charismatic Gifts) [2]

The Charismatic Gifts were given to the church by the Holy Spirit so the body of Christ would be equipped with many extraordinary powers to fulfill their work in His kingdom.

(I Corinthians 12:7-11, Amplified) "But to each one is given the manifestation of the (Holy) Spirit (the evidence, the spiritual illumination of the Spirit) for good and profit. To one is given in and through the (Holy) Spirit (the power to speak) a message of wisdom, and to another (the power to express) a word of knowledge and understanding according to the same (Holy) Spirit. To another (wonder-working) faith by the same (Holy) Spirit, to another the extraordinary powers of healing by the one Spirit. To another the working miracles, to another prophetic insight (the gift of interpreting the divine will and purpose); to another the ability to discern and distinguish between(the utterance of true) spirits (and false ones), to another various kinds of (unknown) tongues, to the ability to interpret (such) tongues. All these (gifts, achievements, abilities) are inspired and brought to pass by one and the same (Holy) Spirit...."

Apostle Paul describes nine of them as "Gifts of Revelation," "Gifts of Power," and "Gifts of Utterance."

   a. Gifts of Revelation (3 parts)

      1. <u>Word of Wisdom</u> – The "gift of wisdom" gives to the body of Christ divine wisdom from the Holy Spirit regarding how to meet a specific need.

      2. <u>Word of Knowledge</u> – The "gift of knowledge" gives to the body of Christ divine knowledge of all things that are relevant to the well-being of the body of Christ.

      3. <u>Discerning of Spirits</u> – The "gift of discerning of spirits" gives to the body of Christ divine revelation of discerning whether certain characteristics of behavior are divine, human, or satanic.

   b. Gifts of Power (3 parts)

      1. <u>Faith</u> – The "gift of faith" is the ability that the Holy Spirit gives to the body of Christ to know with confidence the will and purpose of God for the future of His work. This gift is given for situations needing unquestioning belief that doesn't require proof or evidence.

2. <u>Gift of Healing</u> – The "gift of healing" is a supernatural manifestation of the Holy Spirit given to the body of Christ to meet a need that doesn't restore health or well-being from natural means.

3. <u>Gift of Miracles</u> – The "gift of miracles" is the ability that the Holy Spirit gives to the body of Christ to perform an event or action that apparently contradicts known scientific laws and acts of nature. It's a supernatural act of God.

  c. Gifts of Utterance (3 parts)

1. <u>Gift of Prophecy</u> – The "gift of prophecy" is the ability the Holy Spirit gives to the body of Christ to receive divine inspired messages, prediction of the future under His guidance, and anointed revelation from God.

2. <u>Gift of Tongues</u> – The "gift of tongues" is the ability the Holy Spirit gives believers in the body of Christ to speak a language they have never spoken and build one's self up spiritually, communion with God and when combined with the next gift, makes a message from God for others.

3. <u>Gift of Interpretation of Tongues</u> – The "gift of interpretation of tongues" is the ability the Holy Spirit gives to the body of Christ to make known the message one speaks in tongues. It is a supernatural interpreting of an utterance for the body of Christ.

NOTE: The Charismatic Gifts are more fully explained in a book by Ken Chant, Th.D., *"Equipped to Serve."* If your women's group desires gift testing in this area, contact their ministry for that information. (*Vision Publishing (760) 789-4700 www.visionpublishingservices.com*)

II. <u>Personality Profile</u> – (Temperament and the Christian Faith)

Another tool your women's ministry can use in helping your women develop their callings and giftings is done through teaching "Personality Profile" concepts. These concepts help people examine themselves and become more Christ-like and improve their relationship with others.

(Romans 12:18, Amplified) *"If possible, as far as it depends on you, live at peace with everyone"*

Our temperament is what makes us unique individuals as a part of God's plan. Many counselors (such as Larry Crabb, Gary Smalley, and John Trent) have written books on how the different temperaments give diversity to humans. Their interpretations are different, but their teaching parallels on temperament help our understanding of relationships with one another. Webster's dictionary definition notes the four portions or aspects of temperament as sanguine, phlegmatic, choleric, and melancholic. Let's look at these four temperaments. [3] Note: *"Personality Profile"* (Florence Littauer- Personality evaluation test copies can be ordered by calling 1-800-433-6633 or Vision Publishing 1-800 9VISION)

A. Sanguine (Popular/Influencing)

- Sanguine temperament is usually the easiest to identify, because they tend to be the center of attention, talking the loudest and telling the funniest jokes. Yellow is the color of the sun and their temperament is like the sun shining in the room. They tend to be very cheerful, outgoing and with a very positive outlook on life. They are the ones that tend to be the inspirational leaders of the world and tend to move people emotionally.

- Sanguine temperaments, despite their possessiveness, act as they do in order to receive acceptance and approval. When they don't receive this approval, they become histrionic in style, or even anxiety-driven or neurotic in behavior. They constantly seek attention and when they do not receive it, they may scream, pout, and throw temper tantrums. It they get attention after such behavior, they are rewarded for bad behavior rather than good. This manipulative behavior is learned in their developmental years. More than all other temperaments, they are the most responsive to praise and acceptance or social rewards.

- Sanguine temperaments are not particularly interested in completing tasks, but love to relate to people. When they take on a task, it is done as quickly as possible, so they can return to being with people. They are usually good communicators, talking all the time, wanting to relate to people in an enthusiastic way, yet they still tend to be superficial at times. They will interrupt in mid-sentence others who are speaking, because they desperately feel they have something more important to say. This temperament is constantly active, always looking for something to do, something to keep their minds active. When talking to a sanguine, you will notice that everything negative is a major catastrophe and everything positive is the greatest thing that has ever happened.

- Sanguine temperaments are primarily motivated by love, attention and acceptance, but have difficulty in receiving this at times. While being the life of the party and fun to be with, if the chips are ever down, they are not the type of individual that can be counted on, for they do not tend to be faithful or loyal as friends. Other characteristics include a high degree of impassivity and salesmanship. They will apologize very quickly, which seems sincere, but there is a no real change in behavior. In most areas of life these people tend to be the ones who would say "if it feels good, do it"

    <u>Biblical Character</u> - Apostle Peter seems to be like the Sanguine.

B. Phlegmatic (Peaceful/Sensitive)

- Phlegmatic temperament tends to be slow paced and somewhat stubborn. They can lean toward becoming stagnant, because it takes too much energy to allow their talents to come forth. They tend to do as little as possible in life, and expend as little energy as necessary.

- Phlegmatic temperaments spend most of their time reading books, and think great thoughts. But they rarely share them, so no one would ever know if they did have a brilliant idea. When activities involving others occur, they tend to sit back and observe. They are quite good at judging the heart and motivations of others, yet never do anything themselves. They can work independently day after day with little or no social interactions.

- Phlegmatic temperaments never work hard, yet still have difficulty getting up the next morning. Their humor tends to be dry, their disposition resistive or stubborn. The harder they are pushed to make changes, the more they will resist. To change takes energy, to stay the same doesn't, therefore, they will usually take the path of least resistance.

- Phlegmatic temperaments are task oriented, with a capacity for tasks which are tedious (great bookkeepers, librarians, important papers). Many are authors who write books, do research, and able to stay on tasks for long periods of time without boredom. They think things through well and plan things out meticulously (often laboriously) before accepting social engagements or taking on a task.

- Phlegmatic temperaments can be problematic at times, as they do procrastinate before actually tackling the task. They have the ability to make clear judgments in regard to right and wrong, but they may not know or be willing to do anything about effecting change themselves. They are equally comfortable being an extrovert or introvert, so they can be happy in conversation or just sitting alone with someone they care about. They want peace at any cost. While this makes them easy to get along with, when conflict is necessary to resolve an issue it can also be a problem.
- NOTE: This personality seems to be the only one that can handle the Choleric, because the Choleric cannot control the Phlegmatic. The Phlegmatic has the ability to step aside and out of the way of the controlling influence of the Choleric.

<u>*Biblical Character*</u> *- Martha*

C. Choleric (Powerful/Decisive/Directive)

- The Choleric temperament has the most power and potentially destructive force. They tend to become the strongest leaders in the world. They are interested in power and control and will sometimes use power for negative purposes. They are task oriented and feel the ends justify the means. Their will is persistent.
- Choleric temperaments in social settings can be very personable, optimistic and well liked. They can be charming to the point where people will think of them as the life of the party. However, they do not rely on emotions (love, compassion, tenderness and warmth). Most Cholerics do not see people as human beings to have relationships with, but as objects which can be used for their own benefit.
- Choleric temperaments will tend to do and respond to things according to a specific goal they have in mind, rarely with a concern about how their behavior might affect someone else. A person of this nature will see the goal as the most important thing; whatever it takes to achieve the goal is what they are after. They are driven people. They can be seen in all walks of life, including pastoral ministries.
- Choleric temperaments are often people of vision and yet, because of their aggressive tendencies, may destroy some of the very things they wish to develop. They desperately

want authority and yet have difficulty delegating it, because they have a fear they will be taken advantage of. The color red describes the Choleric, because of their frequently displayed hot tempers. Most Cholerics are well disciplined and efficient. They are organized and will finish the task no matter what it takes.

Biblical Character - *Apostle Paul, after he was saved, became the champion of faith, because God captivated his heart.*

D. Melancholy (Perfect/Controlled)

- Melancholy temperaments tend to have little self-esteem and are indirect in social settings. They can be introverted and unsure of themselves, yet appear competent and in control. They can be friendly and personable, depending on the situation. In clinical terms they lead to depression or mood swings.

- Melancholy temperaments usually use much energy in their thinking. They tend to live in their heads, having a strong desire for intellectual pursuits. They are constantly searching to learn new concepts. They are task oriented rather than relationship oriented. They have a fear of rejection and tend to be rather persistent.

- Melancholy temperaments can be self-sacrificing people. If they think things are about God, they can be very positive in their lives. They seem to be strong willed, but this is probably a defense mechanism against being hurt by others. In relationships they usually do not bond quickly, if they do bond and build relationships, they are a loyal friend for life.

Biblical Character – *Moses, Solomon and John had a melancholy temperament and they discovered great truths and contributed their lives for God.*

In women's ministry, the tools mentioned above can be helpful in developing women for their destiny in the Lord. There are many other outstanding leadership materials available. Listed in Appendix 6 are some other books which have proven most valuable in developing women's ministry.

References:
[1]Marilyn Hickey (1996). *Knowing Your Gift.* Marilyn Hickey Ministry, Denver, Colorado.

[2]Ken Chant (1994). *Equipping to Serve.*, Vision Publishing.

[3]Florence Littauer (Personality Profile). *Personality Evaluation Test.*

[4]Vision Behavioral Profile. Vision Publishing, Ramona, CA

End of Chapter Questions
Chapter 6

1. Discuss the brief history review the author noted regarding the indwelling of the Holy Sprit for believers. Why is this history important for today?
2. List four facts on how to discover your Spiritual Gifts.
3. What are the three Spiritual Gifts categories?
4. List the seven Motivation Gifts and give a brief description of each.
5. List the five-fold Ministry Gifts and give a brief description of them.
6. List the Charismatic Gifts and their three parts and define them.
7. List the four temperaments and describe how understanding them can help in developing relationships.

Part 3

DISCIPLE & DEVELOP LEADERSHIP

"For all these things, My hand has made, and so all these things have come into being (by and for Me), says the Lord. But this is the man to whom I will look and have regard; he who is humble and of a broken or wounded spirit and who trembles at My word and reveres My commands."

(Isaiah 66:2, AMP)

PART 3: Disciple & Develop Leadership

Training leaders is a process. Leadership develops daily, not in a day. Christ is our model and He knew there would be many leaders that would be His messengers in the future. All through Christ's walk He modeled ministry to the world, giving glory to God, demonstrating ways to lead and ways not to lead. He taught in parables and provided them with various experiences preparing them for the future. His model of leadership is servanthood and authority.

"For all these things My hand has made, and so all these things have come into being (by and for Me), says the Lord. But this is the man to whom I will look and have regard; he who is humble and of a broken and wounded spirit, and who trembles at My word and reveres My commands." (Isaiah 66:2)

Successful leaders are learners. It is in their capacity to develop and improve their skills that makes them different from followers. Using Christ as our model, we begin to train leaders by modeling the task at hand. The training you provide for your leaders will be seen in the effectiveness of your ministry. In every women's ministry there needs be a plan as to how to train leaders. In Chapter 5, *"Building Your Leadership Team,"* we presented key elements to be considered that define a leader and also presented characteristics on the development of a leader. These are important in the selection of your leaders. In this chapter we concentrate more on instructional/educational/training to accomplish the task. Preparation for the ministry is a vital part of raising up leaders and we can only do this by properly equipping the saints for this work.

"His intention was the perfecting and the full equipping of the saints (His consecrated people), (that they should do) the work of ministering toward building up Christ's body (the church)." (Ephesians 4:12, Amplified)

In women's ministry there are many instructional/educational/training skills to be learned. They include:

- <u>Christian Foundations</u> - How can a leader minister without knowing Biblical foundational truth?
- <u>Understanding the Biblical View of Women's Role in the Church</u> – What would a leader say, if they weren't knowledgeable about what the Bible says about women?

- <u>Developing Pulpit Ministry</u> – Without developing pulpit ministry training skills, how can a potential leader know how to present a Biblical study, interpretation, or teaching with confidence?

As leaders leading leaders these are important issues to consider in training women to effectively minister in the various areas of service. Let's look at these areas mentioned above in the following chapters.

Chapter 7 *Effective Christian Foundational Training*

Every leader in ministry should have a thorough understanding of basic Christian foundational truths. Many women being ministered to may be confused by the different interpretations of the Bible because of their past belief systems and need to be able to receive solid answers and instruction from their leaders. Because of this issue, one of the first considerations for training of leadership should be basic Biblical foundations.[1]

I. Introduction to Basic Christian Foundations:

*"Therefore, leaving the discussion of the elementary principles of Christ, let us go on to perfection, not laying again the **foundation** of repentance from dead works and of faith toward God, of doctrine of baptisms, of laying on of hands, resurrection of the dead, and of eternal judgment." (Hebrews 6:1-2 NKJ)*

Provided here is a brief outline of what should be taught to ensure an adequate foundation for ministry. The topics to be covered from this foundation Scripture in this class are the six underlined above. As Christians, we need to understand the whole foundation of all six of these principles listed above. All of I Corinthians 3 describes "Foundations for Living" and we are to build upon the foundation that is already laid.

"According to the grace of God which was given to me, as a wise master builder I laid a foundation, and another is building upon it. But let each man be careful how he builds upon it. For no man can lay a foundation other than the one which is laid, which is Jesus Christ. Now if any man builds upon the foundation with gold, silver, precious stones, wood, hay, straw, each man's work will become evident; for the day will show it. Because it is to be revealed with fire, and the fire itself will test the quality of each man's work. If any man's work, which he has built upon it, remains he shall receive a reward. If any man's work is burned up, he shall suffer loss; but he himself shall be saved, yet so as through fire." (1 Corinthians 3:10-15)

The foundation or basis of our life and ministry is truth (God's truth). The Word of God is like a mirror that allows us to see ourselves as we really are and requires hearing and doing what the Word says.

II. Six Foundational Principles

Principle No. 1 - "Repentance from Dead Works"

"Having overlooked the times of ignorance, God is now declaring to men that all men everywhere should repent. (Acts 17:30 NAS)

"From this time Jesus began to preach, and to say, Repent for the kingdom of heaven is at hand." (Matthew 4:17)

A. Definition:
1. Repentance
    a. Meta (Gk)=change
    b. Noieo (Gk)=mind

    Meta-Noieo (To change your mind for the better)

    c. Repentant Heart – (Humility) To see it and do it God's way. An obedient submissive heart to the Word of God, which is the will of God.
2. Dead Works
    a. Nekros (Gk)=dead; devoid of life from God
    b. Ergon (Gk)=toil, effort

    Nekros-Ergon (Lifeless effort)
3. For the Unbeliever
    a. Without repenting they remain separated from Christ *(John 3:17 –18)*
    b. "….because they believe not on me" *(John 16:7-9)*
    c. Therefore there is only one SIN (singular) concerning which God deals with the unbeliever – unbelief toward Christ
    d. When we witness, we must focus on and emphasize the name of Jesus, what He did and who He is.
    e. The unbeliever must change his/her mind about who Christ is.

4. For the Believer
   a. Religious works *(Isaiah 64:6) & (Romans 10"3; "For they being ignorant of God's righteousness, and seeking to establish their own righteousness, have not submitted to the righteousness of God."*
   b. Works of the flesh *(Galatians 5:19-21)*
   c. Fruitless suffering under delusion of spiritual value (sickness, poverty, family problems, calamities, etc.)
   d. Lack of zeal for Christ, first love *(Revelation 2:4-5 "But I have this against you, that you have left your first love. Remember therefore from where you have fallen, and repent and do the deeds you did at first; or else I am coming to you, and will remove your lampstand out of its place –unless you repent") & (Philippians 3:8-15).*
   e. The believer must <u>change</u> their mind about these things.
   f. The change is always evidenced in three elements.

Element	Evidence	Prodigal Son Luke 15:11-32
Intellectual (Mind)	Change of Thinking	*"He came to his senses"*
Emotional (Emotions)	Change of Heart	*"I have sinned....."*
Volitional (Will)	Change of Choices	*"I will get up and go to my father."*

B. The "How To" of Repentance
   1. The Fear of the Lord is a respect for God *(I Corinthians 6:19-20)*
      a. Dreadful displeasure of displeasing God – right attitude toward God.
      b. Hatred of unrighteousness *(Proverbs 6:13)*
      c. The beginning of wisdom and knowledge *(Proverbs 1:7 "The fear of the Lord is the beginning of knowledge, fools despise wisdom and instruction") & (Psalm 111:10 "For the fear of the Lord is the beginning of wisdom, and the knowledge of the holy One is understanding."*
      d. Can be learned *(Psalm 34:11 "Come you children, listen to me; I will teach you the fear of the Lord.")*
      e. Crucial to repentance and receiving correction *(Proverbs 16:6)*

2. Elements of repentance (Three "C"s)
   a. Conviction - II Corinthians 7:10 *"For godly sorrow produces repentance leading to salvation, not to be regretted, but the sorrow of the world produces death")*
   b. Confession - Refer to: II Samuel, Job 33:27; & I John 1:8-9 *"If we say that we have no sin, we deceive ourselves, and the truth is not in us. If we confess our sins, He is faithful and just to forgive us our sins and to cleanse us from all unrighteousness."*
   c. Conversion - (change in conduct)
      1. Grace is imparted when we humble ourselves
      James 4:6 "But He gives a greater grace, therefore it says, God is opposed to the proud, but gives grace to the humble")
      2. Grace is the ability to think and act differently
   d. Roadblock – Besetting sins can be broken through bringing another brother to our confession. *(James 5:16 "Therefore, confess your sins to one another, and pray for one another, so that you may be healed. The effective prayer of a righteous man can accomplish much.")*
3. Frequency of Repentance
   1. Brother to brother – 70x7 *(Matthew 18:22)*
   2. Must be a lifestyle
   3. Repentance is the first foundational doctrine
4. False Repentance
   a. Remorse *(Matthew 27:3-4 – Judas returning the thirty pieces of silver.)*
   b. Sorrow for being caught *(Worldly sorrow)*
   c. Sorrow for not wanting to change *(Matthew 19:22 – To give up what you have.)*

Summarizing "Principle No 1" – This is a good place to take a few minutes to pray, reflecting on your life, and if the Holy Spirit has illuminated areas that need to be repented of, confess and receive forgiveness. Let the Lord minister His forgiveness and grace to the people.

Principle No. 2 - <u>Faith Toward God</u>
   A. Two Kinds of Faith

1. By works of the law *(Deuteronomy 6:25* – Doesn't actually work*)* & *(Romans 3:20, "Because by the works of the Law no flesh will be justified in His sight; for through the law comes the knowledge of sin.")*
2. By faith, not by works *"Ephesians 2:9, "For by grace you have been saved through faith; and that not of yourselves, it is the gift of God; not as a result of works, that no one should boast.")* & *(II Corinthians 5:21, "He made Him who knew no sin to be sin on our behalf that we might become the righteousness of God in Him.")*
3. Who then is righteous? *(Romans 4:22-24)* & *(Heb. 2:4)*
4. We must "renew our minds" to righteousness by faith

B. The Breastplate of Righteousness
1. Defensive armor is spiritual warfare *(Ephesians 6:14)*
2. Also called "breastplate of faith and love." *(I Thessalonians 5:8, "But since we are of the day, let us be sober, having put on the breastplate of faith and love, and as a helmet, the hope of salvation.")*
3. Satan's tactic is to assault our "righteousness consciousness" through the weapons of condemnation *(Romans 8:1)* and accusation. *(Revelation 2:10, ".....for the accuser of our brethren has been thrown down, who accuses them before our God day and night.")*
4. We must resist him, or faith and love will not flow through our lives. *(they issue from the heart- protected by the breastplate.)*

C. Faith Facts
1. Definition – *(Hebrews 11:1, "Now faith is the assurance (substance) of things hoped for, and the conviction (evidence) of things not seen.")*
2. Development of our faith *(Romans 12:3, "dealt a measure of faith")* & *(Romans 10:17, "faith comes from hearing and hearing by the word of Christ.")*
3. Meditation in the Word of God, "like a cow chewing grass," we "chew" the Word (mutter-read out load repeatedly, with a heart to receive). *(Joshua 1:8)*
4. Like a seed, it is planted. (Parables of "sower" and "Man who cast seed"). *(Mark 4:14-20, 24)*
5. Faith sees and knows *(Hebrews 11:27, "By faith Moses left Egypt, not fearing the wrath of the king; for he endured, as seeing Him who is unseen.');* <u>knows</u> *(Hebrews*

11:1); speaks (II Corinthians 4:13, (Paul) "But having the same spirit of faith according to what is written, 'I believe, therefore I spoke' we also believe, therefore also we speak."); receive (Mark 11:24, "Therefore I say to you, all things for which you pray and ask, believe that you have received them, and they shall be granted you."); obeys "By faith Abraham, when he was called, obeyed by going out to a place which he was to receive for an inheritance; and he went out, not knowing where he was going."; and acts (James 2:17, "Even so, faith, if it has no works, is dead, being by itself."

6. Words are powerful *(Proverbs 18:21, "Death and life are in the power of the tongue."*

D. Purposes of Faith

1. To receive *(Mark 11:24)* the promises of God
2. To give *(Matthew 10:8, "Heal the sick, raise the dead, cleanse the lepers, cast out demons, freely you receive, freely give.") & (Philemon 1:6)*
3. To fulfill our destiny in God *(Psalm 37:1-4, "Trust in the Lord, and do good; dwell in the land and cultivate faithfulness. Delight yourself in the Lord; and He will give you the desires of your heart. Commit your way to the Lord, trust also in Him, and He will do it.")*

E. The Trail of Faith

1. Your faith will be challenged; it has enemies
2. Passivity negates faith *(Matthew 11:12)*
3. Doubt can be cast down *(II Corinthians 10:3-5, "For though we walk in the flesh, we do not war according to the flesh, for the weapons of our warfare are not carnal, but mighty in God for pulling down strongholds, casting down arguments and every high thing that exalts itself against the knowledge of God, bringing every thought into captivity to the obedience of Christ.")*
4. Abraham's example *(Romans 4:26-22)*

Summarizing "Principle No. 2" – "Faith" is the fuel that energizes the "Fact" (Word of God) and gives it life. After studying these facts, we need to take time to pray and thank God for increasing our "Faith," because we have heard His Word and see how it can energize us.

Principle No. 3 – "Baptisms"

"But he who is joined to the Lord is one spirit with Him. (vs17)……"Or do you not know that your body is the temple of the Holy Spirit who is in you, whom you have from God, and you are not your own? For you were bought at a price; therefore glorify God in your body and in your spirit, which are God's". (I Corinthians 6: 17; 19-20, NKJ)

The "New Birth" is a "Double Birth." Baptism means an act or experience by which one is purified, sanctified (set apart).

   A. Baptized into Christ – When we believe in and receive Jesus Christ as Lord and Savior.

      1. Identification with Christ *(John 12:32, "And I, if and when I am lifted up from the earth (on the cross), will draw and attract all men (Gentiles as well as Jews) to myself.") & (II Corinthians 5:17, " Therefore if any person is (ingrafted) in Christ (the Messiah) he is a new creation (a new creature altogether); the old lresh (previous moral and spiritual condition) has passed away. Behold the flesh and new has come.")*

      2. Into His death *(Romans 6:3, Paul said to the people regarding sin/grace, "Are you ignorant of the fact that all of us who have been baptized into Christ Jesus were baptized into His death?")*

      3. Buried and raised with Him *(Galatians 2:20) & (Romans 6:4, "We were buried therefore with Him by the baptism into death, so that just as Christ was raised from the dead by the glorious (power) of the Father so we too might (habitually) live and behave in newness of life.")*

   B. Baptized into Christ's Body – Set apart by God's Spirit

      1. Identification with Christ's Body. The Holy Spirit baptizes the believer into the body which is the church. *(I Corinthians 12:13, "For by one spirit we were all baptized into one body – whether Jews or Greeks – whether slaves or free – and have all been made to drink into one Spirit.")*

      2. This is the one baptism spoken of in Ephesians 4:5 (the context of Ephesians 4:1-6 is oneness in the church). *(Ephesians 4:5 "One Lord, One Faith, One Baptism.")*

      3. This baptism…

a. Produces the believer's oneness with other believers, fulfilling Jesus' high priestly prayer of John 17. Prayers Christ prayed before being arrested.
   b. A proof of the new birth *(I John 3:14, "We know that we have passed from death to life, because we love the brethren. He who does not love his brother abides in death.")*

"Baptism in Water"

A. Baptism in Water is a Commandment
   1. John the Baptist baptized *(Matthew 3:6)*
   2. Jesus' followers were baptized in water by immersion *(John 3:22)*
   3. Jesus, Himself, was water baptized *(Matthew 3:16)*
   4. Jesus assumed that those who would believe on Him would also be water baptized. *(Mark 16:15-16)*
   5. Peter commanded New Testament converts to be baptized in water *(Acts 2:38; 10:48)* & *(Mark 16:15-16 "And He said to them, Go into all the world and preach and publish openly the good news (the Gospel) to every creature (of the whole human race. He who believes (who adheres to and trusts in and relies on the Gospel and him whom it sets forth) and is baptized will be saved (from the penalty of eternal death); but he who does not believe (who does not adhere to and trust in and rely on the Gospel and Him whom it sets forth) will be condemned.*

B. Follows The New Birth
   1. Not valid if occurs before the new birth *(Acts 19:1-7)*
   2. Immersion is the Biblical pattern. Examples: *(Acts 8:36-39), (Matthew 3:16), (Mark 1:10), (John 3:23)*
   3. Infant baptism is not taught in the Bible. The person must repent and believe.

C. Purpose
   1. Not to remove Sin *(Hebrews 9:14)*, because it's by the blood of Christ that our conscience is purged.
   2. Act of obedience *(Matthew 28:19, "Go therefore and make disciples of all nations, baptizing them into the name of the Father, the Son, and the Holy Spirit.")*
   3. An act of solidarity, which means unity based on (Biblical) standard, both with Christ and with the church.

"Baptism with the Holy Spirit"

- A. Pattern for Believers
    1. The 120 were baptized with the Holy Spirit in the Upper Room.   *(Acts 2:1-4)*
    2. Other cases in Acts:
        a. Samaritans *(Acts 8:15-17)*
        b. Paul *(I Corinthians 14:18)*
        c. House of Cornelius *(Acts 10:44-47)*
        d. Ephesians *(Acts 19:6)*
- B. Who Is It For?
    1. Born again persons have the Holy Spirit, *(John 20:21-22, Jesus appeared to the Disciples and said: 'Peace to you as the Father has sent me. I also send you and when he had said this, He breathed on them, and said to them, Receive the Holy Spirit");* like a well, *(Isaiah 12:3,"Therefore with joy you will draw water from the wells of salvation".)* & *(John 4:14, "But whoever drinks of the water that I shall give him will never thirst, but the water that I shall give him will become in him a fountain of water springing up into everlasting life.")*
    2. Born again persons need the Holy Spirit like a river *(John 7:37-39)*, upon them.
    3. Don't have to "tarry" nor be "mature."
    4. Simply ask and believe, *(Luke 11:13, "If you then, being evil know how to give good gifts to your children, how much more will your heavenly Father give the Holy Spirit to those who ask Him.")* The same simple faith that saved you, is the same way you receive the Baptism of the Holy Spirit; don't reason, just believe and receive.
    5. It's the promise of the Father *(Acts 1:4-5, "He commanded them not to depart from Jerusalem, but to wait for the Promise of the Father which he said, 'You have heard from me,, for truly John baptized with water, but you shall be baptized with the Holy Spirit not many days from now"), (Acts 2:38-39),* for all who believe. *(Mark 16:17)*
    6. Power to fulfill purpose *(Acts 1:8, "You shall receive power when the Holy Spirit comes upon you and you shall be witnesses to Me in Jerusalem and in all Judea and Samaria and to the end of the Earth.")*

C. Evidence
  1. Not emotions
  2. Not the fruit of the Holy Spirit (evident with New Birth). *(Galatians 5:22-23)*
  3. Evidence is speaking in tongues. *(Acts 10:45-46, "And those of the circumcision who believed were astonished as many as came with Peter, because of the gift of the Holy Spirit had been poured out on the Gentiles, For they heard them speak with tongues and magnify God.")*
     a. Tongues as a prayer language *(Romans 8:26-28, "Likewise the Spirit also helps in our weaknesses. For we do not know what we should pray for as we ought, but the Spirit Himself makes intercessions for us with groanings which cannot be uttered. Now He who searches the hearts knows what the mind of the Spirit is, because he makes intercession for the saints according to the will of God")*, helps you to pray according to God's will.
     b. Tongues as a gift of the Holy Spirit *(I Corinthians 12:10, Referring to the Diversity of the Gifts: "To another the working of miracles, to another prophecy, to another discerning of spirits, to another different kinds of tongues…")* is to be used with interpretation when it is a message for the church.
     c. Tongues of men, or tongues of (heavenly) angels. *(I Corinthians 13:10)*
        (1) Have heard of missionaries speaking in tongues and it being the tongue of the people they were speaking to and they didn't know the language as in *Acts 2*.
        (2) Heavenly "tongue of angels" when praying according to God's will as in *(Romans 8:26-28)*.
  4. Supernatural - God does the "super," you do the "natural."
D. Purpose
  1. Upward purpose – worship *(John 4:23-24, "But the hour is coming and now is when the true worshippers will worship the Father in spirit and truth; for the Father is seeking such to worship Him. God is Spirit, and those who worship Him must worship in spirit and truth.")*
  2. Inward purpose – edification *(I Corinthians 14:5, "I wish you all spoke with tongues, but even more that you prophesied; for he who prophesies is greater than he who speaks with tongues, unless indeed he interprets, that the church may*

receive edification"); builds your faith *(Jude 1:20);* helps you to pray according to the perfect will of God when you may not know what to pray *(Romans 8:26-28);* rest and refreshing *(Isaiah 28: 11-12)*

3. Outward purpose – boldness as witnesses *(Acts 1:8)*

<u>"Baptism With Suffering"</u> *(Matthew 20:22-23) & (Mark 10:38)*

A. Persecution is Real
   1. Jesus suffered
      a. Our example - in His life (Luke 4:28-30)
      b. Our substitute in His death *(Romans 5:6-8, "For when we were still without strength, in due time Christ died for the ungodly. For scarcely for a righteous man will one die, yet perhaps for a good man someone would even dare to die; But God demonstrates His own love toward us, in that while we were still sinners Christ died for us") & (Mark:33-38) & (Luke 12:50).*
   2. Comes through people *(John 16:2)*
   3. Inspired by Satan *(II Corinthians 4:4) & (I Thessalonians 2:18, "We wanted to come to you, but Satan hindered us.")*
   4. Comes to believers *(II Timothy 3:12, "All who desire to live godly in Christ Jesus will suffer persecution") & (John 15:20).*
   5. Comes in seasons *(I Peter 5:10, "But the God of all grace, who called us to His eternal glory by Christ Jesus, after you have suffered a while, perfect, establish, strengthen, and settle you") & (I Peter 1:6, "In this you greatly rejoice, though now for a little while, if need be, you have been grieved by various trials.")*
   6. Varies in intensity *(Psalm 34:19, "Many are the afflictions of the righteous, but the Lord delivers him out of them all.")*
   7. God is working – He will deliver *(Psalm 34:19, "Many are the afflictions of the righteous, but the Lord delivers him out of them all.") & (II Timothy 3:10-11)*

B. Two Causes of Persecution
   1. Persecuted for righteousness sake, for being salt. *(Matthew 5:19-16, "...vs16 Let your light so shine before men, that they may see your good works and glorify your Father in heaven."*

2. Persecuted for the gospel's sake, for being light.*(Matthew 5:19-16, "...vs14 "You are the light of the world, A city that is set on a hill cannot be hidden....."*

C. How to Handle Persecution

1. Remember Jesus (Hebrews 12:1-4)
2. Keep a good testimony (II Timothy 4:14-18, Amplified), be faithful
3. Don't look for it (Matthew 10:23)
4. Look for a way out (I Corinthians 10:13, Amplified); (Luke 4:1-13)
5. Forgive (Matthew 5:44), love and pray
6. Let God judge (II Thessalonians 1:6)
7. Resist the devil (James 4:6-8)
8. Rejoice (Acts 5:4)
9. Fear not (Luke 12:4-5)
10. Count the cost (Luke 14:26-35)

Correct Godly responses to persecution:

- Love and Pray
- Speak the Word
- Rejoice
- Don't Fear
- God will take care of it
- Be patient and God will deliver you

Principle No. 4 – **The Laying on of Hands**

The Anointing

A. Definition – Manifest, active presence of the Spirit of God in or upon a person or persons.

B. Purpose of the Anointing

"The Spirit of the Lord is upon Me, because He has anointed Me (the Anointed One, the Messiah) to <u>preach the good news (the gospel) to the poor</u>; He has sent Me to announce <u>release to the captives</u> and <u>recovery of sight to the blind</u>, to send forth as <u>delivered those who are oppressed (who are downtrodden, bruised, crushed, and broken down by calamity</u>." (Luke 4:18, Amplified)

1. Preach the gospel to the poor
2. Release to the captives
3. Recovery of sight to the blind
4. Deliverance for the oppressed, downtrodden, bruised, crushed and those broken down by calamity.

C. Qualities of the Anointing *(Mark 5:29-30, "Immediately the fountain of her blood was dried up, and she felt in her body that she was healed of the affliction....") & (Luke 6:19, "And the whole multitude sought to touch Him, for power went out from Him and healed them all.")*

1. Tangible
2. Transmittable
3. Receivable

<u>The Laying on of Hands</u>

A. Purpose – To transfer the anointing.
1. For healing and deliverance *((Mark 5:41; 6:5; 7:32-33; 8:22-25; 16:17-18) & (Luke 40:40-41; 13:10-13)*
2. For the baptism in the Holy Spirit *(Acts 8:17, "Then they laid hands on them and they received the Holy Spirit."*
3. Confirm ministries in the church *(I Timothy 4:14; 5:22) & (II Timothy 1:6, "Therefore I remind you to stir up the gift of God which is in you through the laying on of my hands.")*

B. Who May Practice the Laying on of Hands?
1. Believers
   a. For healing *(Mark 16:16-18, "He who believes and is baptized will be saved; but he who does not believe will be condemned. And these signs will follow those who believe. In My name they will cast out demons; they will speak with new tongues. They will take up serpents, and if they drink anything deadly it will by no means hurt them; they will lay hands on the sick and they will recover.")*
   b. For the baptism *(Acts 9:17-18, Saul filled with the Spirit: "And Ananias went his way and entered the house; and laying his hands on him he said,*

'Brother Saul, the Lord Jesus, who appeared to you on the road as you came, has sent me that you may receive your sight and be filled with the Holy Spirit. Immediately there fell from his eyes something like scales, and he received his sight at once; and he arose and was baptized."

    2. Church Leadership

        a. Deacons *(Acts 6:1-6)*

        b. Ministers *(Acts 13:1-3)*

        c. Warning *(I Timothy 5:22)*

    3. The ministry in the church service – designated people

Principle No. 5 <u>**Resurrection of the Dead**</u>

<u>Importance of the doctrine</u> – Must believe in the Resurrection

    A. Christ's Own Resurrection

        a. Jesus rose from the dead *(I Corinthians 15:3-8)* & *(Acts 2:24, "But God raised Him from the dead, freeing Him from the agony of death, because it was impossible for death to keep its hold on Him.")*

        b. If not true, then we are still sinners *(I Corinthians 15:12-17)* & *(Romans 4:25, "But also for us, it shall be imputed to us who believe in Him who raised up Jesus our Lord from the dead.")*

        c. He is the firstfruits *(I Corinthians 15:20-23,………vs22 "For as in Adam all die, so in Christ all will be made alive. But each in his own turn; Christ, the firstfruits; afterward who He comes, those who belong to Him."*

    B. Our Hope: The Resurrection of the Believer

      1. Bodily redemption is our hope *((Romans 8:23-24, "……We groan inwardly as we wait eagerly for our adoption as sons, the redemption of our bodies."*

      2. This hope purifies us *(I John 3:2-3, "Dear friends, now we are children of God, and what we will be has not yet been made known. But we know that when He appears, we shall be like Him, for we shall see Him as He is. Everyone who has this hope in Him purifies himself, just as He is pure.")*

      3. This hope is the anchor of our soul *(Hebrews 6:19, "This hope we have as an anchor of the soul, both sure and steadfast, and which enters the presence behind the veil")*.

4. This hope is part of our spiritual defensive armor *(Ephesians 6:17 & (I Thessalonians 5:8, "....putting on faith and love as a breastplate, and the hope of salvation as a helmet.")*

C. The Doctrine that Awakens the Sinner

1. Christ's resurrection provides for Christ's return *(Acts 1:11, "...This same Jesus, who has been taken from you into heaven, will come back in the same way, you have seen Him go into heaven.")*

2. Apostles preached the resurrection *(Acts 1:22; 2:32; 17:30-32; 4:33, "With great power the apostles continued to testify to the resurrection of the Lord Jesus, and much grace was upon them all."*

3. If no resurrection, then no fear of God and no moral code *(I Corinthians 15:32 "...If the dead are not raised, 'Let us eat, and drink for tomorrow we die.'")*

4. An essential part of the gospel message *(I Corinthians 15:42-44, 49-58)*.

Confusion Surrounding This Doctrine

A. Jewish Resistance

1. The Sadducees denied the resurrection *(Mark 12:18-27, "Then the Sadducees, who say there is no resurrection, came to Him with a question, (Whose wife will this woman be? She had been married seven times), Jesus answered: vs 25 'When the dead rise, they will neither marry nor be given in marriage; they will be like the angels in heaven.'"*

2. Jewish leaders paid the guards to lie about Christ's body (and they did) *(Matthew 28:11-25, "......vs 13 "Tell the people His disciples came at night and stole Him away while we were sleeping.")*

B. Various Heresies Among the Church

1. Some have said it already is past *(II Timothy 2:18, "....Who have strayed concerning the truth, saying that the resurrection is already past; and they overthrow the faith of some")*, (upsetting the faith of some).

2. Individual super-spirituality

3. The dualism of Gnostics (matter is evil; spirit is good) – Don't believe that Jesus came in the flesh.

4. Jehovah's witnesses teach selective resurrection; some will cease to exist.
5. New Age believes God exists in everything.

C. Non-Church Error

1. Reincarnation *(Hebrews 9:27, "Just as man is destined to die once, and after that to face judgment, so Christ was sacrificed once to take away the sins of many people....")*
2. Astral projection; some have not returned.
3. Society has increasing curiosity.

The Truth About Death

A. Things Common to All Men

1. All are eternal, spirit beings made in the image of God. *(Genesis 1:26, "Let Us make man in Our image.")* & *(I Thessalonians 5:23, "May your whole spirit, soul and body be kept blameless...."*
2. At death, the spirit and soul leave the body. *(II Corinthians 5:8)* & *(Ecclesiastes 12:7, "...and the dust returns to the ground it came from, and the spirit returns to God who gave it.")*
3. At death, eternal destiny is already determined *(John 3:18)* & *(Hebrews 9:27, "And as it is appointed for men to die one, but after this the judgment.")*

B. The Death of the Righteous

1. Before Christ's own resurrection
    a. Abraham's bosom *(Luke 16:22, "And it came to pass, that the beggar died, and was carried by the angels into Abraham's bosom: the rich man also died, and was buried...")* Abraham's bosom is a separate compartment in the great pit at the heart of the earth.
    b. Or Paradise *(Luke 23:42-43, ".......and Jesus said to him, 'Assuredly I say to you, today you will be with Me in Paradise.")*
2. At Christ's resurrection, paradise was moved *(Ephesians 4:8); (I Peter 3:18-20); and Matthew 27:52-53.)*

C. The Death of the Wicked and the Sinner

1. Descent to region of Hades (Greek) or Sheol (Hebrew) *(Luke 16:19-31)*

2. Torment *(Matthew 13:41-43, 49-50,* as well as other Scriptures) weeping, wailing and gnashing of teeth. *(Mark 9:48), (Isaiah 66:24)* Worm dies not, and the fire is not quenched. *(Revelation 21:8)* which burns with fire and brimstone (sulfur).

<u>The Truth About Resurrection</u>

A. Some will be raised to a resurrection of life, others to a resurrection of damnation. *(John 5:28-20, "......the hour is coming, in which all that are in the graves shall hear His voice, and shall come forth; they that have done good, unto the resurrection of life, and they that have done evil, unto the resurrection of damnation.")*

B. The Resurrection of the Righteous

  1. A reuniting of the spirit and soul with the resurrected body.

  2. The resurrected body is flesh and bone, incorruptible, glorified, spiritual, heavenly, immortal, perfect and raised in power *(I Corinthians 15:42-44,49),* as was the body of Jesus Christ when He arose *(Luke 24:39, "Behold my hands and my feet, that it is I myself; handle me, and see; for a spirit does not have flesh and bones, as you see Me have"; & verses 42-45.*

C. The Rapture

  1. Scripture distinguishes:...

    a. The moment Christ comes FOR His church is called the Rapture.

    b. The moment He comes WITH His church *(Revelation 1:7; Zechariah 14:5),* is also called the second coming or second advent.

  2. Not a Biblical term, but implied in many Scriptures – for example: *(I Thessalonians 4:13-18.........vs. 17) "Then we which are alive and remain shall be caught up together with them in the clouds, to meet the Lord in the air...."* <u>harpazo</u> (Greek) means 'caught up.' The English word 'rapture' comes from the Latin <u>*raptus*</u>, meaning 'seized' or 'carried away.'

  3. Will involve the whole family of God in heaven (believers which are "asleep" in Jesus) and on the earth (we, which are alive and remain).

  4. Desirable to escape tribulation wrath (Luke 21:34-36)

  5. Beliefs vary as to "pre-tribulation," "mid-tribulation," and post -tribulation" rapture.

    a. *(II Timothy 2:33 -36)* says not to argue this or be in strife.

    b. *(Matthew 24:42, 44)* says to be ready.

c. *Matthew 24:36),* says no one knows the exact day or hour.

D. The Resurrection of the Wicked and the Sinner

1. A single event
2. Discussed in *(Revelation 20:5, 12-13)*
3. Follows the millennium *(Revelation 20:1-15)*
4. Is preparatory to their judgment

Principle No. 6 <u>Eternal Judgment</u>

<u>God is the Judge of All</u>

A. God Made Everything

1. God made the angels *(Psalm 148:2, "Praise Him all His angels,...vs5. Let them praise the name of the Lord; for He commanded, and they were created.") & (Ezekiel 18:4)*
2. God made the heavens and the earth *(Genesis 1:1)*
3. God finished the heavens and the earth *(Genesis 1:1-25)*
4. God made man *(Genesis 1:26-31; 5:1)*

B. God Owns Everything

1. The universe *(Psalm 115:16, "The heavens are the Lord's, but the earth He has given to the children of men.")*
2. The earth is the Lord's and the world *(Psalm 24:1, "The earth is the Lord's and the fullness of it; the world and they that dwell therein.")*
3. All souls are the Lord's *(Ezekiel 6:4, "Behold all souls are mine...")*

C. God is the Judge of All

1. God judged the angels that fell *(Jude 6)*
2. God is the judge of all men *(II Timothy 4:1, "...and the Lord Jesus Christ, who shall judge the quick (living in Christ) and the dead (never made alive in Christ) at His appearing and His kingdom") & (Hebrews 12:22-23).*

<u>Man is Accountable to God</u>

A. God Gave Man Life

1. He breathed into man's nostrils the breath of life *(Genesis 2)*

2. Man became a living soul *(Genesis 2:7, "And the Lord God formed man of the dust of the ground, and breathed into his nostrils the breath of life; and man became a living being.")*

B. God Established Standards of Good and Evil
1. Lost man has a conscience to know right from wrong
   a. The woman taken in adultery *(John 8:9, "...being convicted by their own conscience...")*
   b. Those who don't have the law do that which is in the law *(Romans 2:14-15)*
2. Born again person receives a clean conscience
   a. The blood of Christ cleanses our conscience from dead works *(Hebrews 9:14 "How much more shall the blood of Christ, who through the eternal Spirit offered Himself without spot to God, cleanse your conscience from dead works to serve the living God.")*
   b. We are accountable to keep our conscience clean by confessing our sins. *(I John 1:9, "If we confess our sins, He is faithful and just to forgive us our sins, and to cleanse us from all unrighteousness.")*
3. Jesus said the Holy Spirit is in the world to convince man in three areas.
   a. "Sin – because they believe not on me."
   b. "Righteousness – because I go to My Father."
   c. "Judgment – because the prince of this world is judged."

Eternal Judgment

A. What is Eternal Judgment
1. God will judge every person on the basis of the life they lived.*(Romans 14:9-12, "....vs12 "so then each of us shall give account of himself to God...")*
2. It is eternal, because it can never be changed.
3. Both the righteousness and the sinner will be judged. *(II Corinthians 5:10, "For we must all appear before the judgment seat of Christ, that each one may receive the things done in the body, according to what he has done, whether good or bad.")*

B. Who Executes Judgment
1. The father has authority to judge. *(John 5:26-27)*
2. The father has given all judgment to the Son. *(John 5:22-23)*

3. The basis for judgment is the Word of God. *(John 12:48, "He who rejects Me, and does not received My words, has that which judges him – the word that I have spoken will judge him in the last day.")*

C. What is the Basis of Judgment

1. Judgment will be according to truth. *(John 12:48)* & *(Romans 12:1-2)*
2. Judgment will be according to works. *(Romans 2:6-9)*; *(I Corinthians 3:11-15)*; *(Revelation 20:13, "....And they will be judged, each one according to his works.")*
3. Judgment will be impartial. *(Romans 2:6-11)*
4. Judgment will be according to conscience. *(Romans 2:12-15, "....their conscience also bearing witness, and between themselves their thoughts accusing or else excusing them.")*
5. Judgment will be according to the secrets of the heart. *(Romans 2:16, "Do you not know that to whom you present yourselves slaves to obey, whether of sin leading to death, or of obedience leading to righteousness.")*

The Central Event of History

A. Christ Suffered in Place of Every Person

1. Jesus Christ, the Son of God, was nailed to a common Roman cross for six hours.
2. The sins of the world were laid upon Him. *(Isaiah 53:6, "All we like sheep have gone astray; We have turned, every one, to his own way; and the Lord has laid on Him the iniquity of us all.")*
3. The blood of the Lamb of God was shed to remove men's sins.
4. God executed judgment against the whole human race in Christ. *(II Corinthians 5:21, "For He made Him who knew no sin to be sin for us, that we might become the righteousness of God in Him.)*
5. Jesus is a type of the serpent in the wilderness *(John 3:14-15, "And as Moses lifted up the serpent in the wilderness, even so must the Son of Man be lifted up, that whoever believes in Him should not perish, but have eternal life*

B. Response to the Gospel

1. The gospel must be preached. *(II Corinthians 5:11, "Knowing, therefore, the terror of the Lord, we persuade men; but we are well known to God, and I also trust are well known in your consciences."*

2. Men escaped the wrath of God by believing the gospel.
3. God's will is that no one perish *(John 3:6) & (II Peter 3-9,"The Lord is not slack concerning His promise, as some count slackness, but is long suffering toward us, not willing that any should perish but that all should come to repentance.")*
4. Men inherit the wrath of God by not coming to the light. *(John 3:18-20)*

<u>The Judgment of the Wicked and Sinners</u>

A. The Great White Throne (*Revelation 20:11-15*)
1. It takes place after the millennium.
2. They will be resurrected.
3. The books will be opened.
4. They will be judged according to their works.
5. They will be cast into the lake of fire (Greek =gehenna)
6. *(Revelation 21:8, "But the cowardly, unbelieving, abominable, murders, sexually immoral, sorcerers, idolaters, and all liars shall have their part in the lake which burns with fire and brimstone, which is the second death."*
7. The heavens and the earth will burn up, and God will create a new heaven and a new earth. *(Revelation 21:1, "Now I saw a new heaven and a new earth, for the first heaven and the first earth had passed away…")*

<u>The Judgment of the Believers</u>

A. A Judgment of Fire
4. The believers' works will pass through fire. *(I Corinthians 3:13, "…for the Day will declare it, because it will be revealed by fire; and the fire will test each one's work, of what sort it is."*
5. Works will be classified. *(I Corinthians 3:11-13, "For no other foundation can anyone lay than that which is laid, which is Jesus Christ. Now if anyone builds on this foundation with gold, silver, precious stones, wood, hay, straw, each one's work will become clear ….")*
    a. Wood, hay, and stubble
    b. Gold, silver and precious stones
4. This shows that God is looking for quality, not quantity.

5. If the works are still there after passing through the fire, there will be a reward. *(I Corinthians 3:14, "If anyone's work which he has built on it endures, he will receive a reward.")*

6. There will be a consciousness of a loss suffered for works not rewarded. *(I Corinthians 3:15, "if anyone's work is burned, he will suffer loss; but he himself will be saved, yet so as through fire.")*

B. What is a Quality Work

  1. Motive should be Godly

    a. For whose glory? Mine or God's? *(Matthew 6:1, "Don't do good deeds to be seen of men or you will have no reward in heaven for them.*

    b. The love of God. *(I Corinthians 13:3)*

  2. Motive should be obedience

    a. *(Proverbs 14:12, "There is a way that seems right to a man, but the end are the ways of death.")* Prayer should be the origination.

    b. *(Isaiah 1:19, "If you be willing and obedient...")*

    c. We have been given commandments.

  3. Motive should be faithfulness

    a. God has given us many talents, gifts, and resources.

    b. We should be faithful with them.

      1. Money
      2. Time
      3. Revelation in the Word
      4. Talents and abilities
      5. Relationships
      6. Opportunities

C. Some Things that are Specifically Rewarded

  1. Preaching the Gospel *(I Corinthians 9:16-17)*

  2. Suffering persecution cheerfully *(Matthew 5:12, "Rejoice and be exceedingly glad, for great is your reward in heaven, for so they persecuted the prophets who were before you."*

  3. Using talents and gifts in God's service. *(Luke 19:11-27)*

  4. Showing love to one's enemies. *(Matthew 5:38-48)*

  5. Ministry to people *(Matthew 10:41-42)*, including hospitality, *(Luke 14:12-14)*

6. Fulfilling one's normal, daily scriptural responsibilities as unto the Lord. *(Colossians 3:18-25)*

D. Crowns

1. There is an incorruptible crown. *(I Corinthians 9:19-27)*
2. There is a crown of rejoicing. *(I Thessalonians 2:19-20, "For what is our hope, or joy, or crown of rejoicing? Is it not even you in the presence of our Lord Jesus Christ at His coming? For you are our glory and our joy")*
3. There is a crown of righteousness. *(II Timothy 4:7-8, I have fought the good fight, I have finished the race, I have kept the faith. Finally, there is laid up for me the crown of righteousness, which the Lord, the righteous Judge, will give to me at that day and not to me only, but also to all who have loved His appearing.")*
4. There is a crown of life. *(Revelation 2:10)* & *(James 1:12, "Blessed is the man who endures temptation; for when he has been approved, he will receive the crown of life which the Lord has promised to those who love Him.")*
5. There is the crown of glory. *(I Peter 5:1-4)*
6. Leave the rewards up to God. *(Matthew 19:27; 20:16)* & *(I Corinthians 9:24, "Do you not know that those who run in a race all run, but one receives the prize? Run in such a way that you may obtain it."*

References:

[1] Derived from *Foundation Stones*, Resurrection Life Church, Grandville, MI

End of Chapter Questions –

Chapter 7

There are six Foundational Principles. Define each Principle and write a brief summary of each.

Chapter 8 *Understanding the Historical View of Women's Roles*

Women in ministry should learn and understand the historical view of women's role in the church. In the past, our understanding of the Bible has been obtained from the interpretations and translations of Church Fathers who guarded the Canon of Holy Writ. Today we have greater access to historical documents and language usage, which provide many different interpretations from long established ones. One of those Biblical misinterpretations is of the word *"head."* Headship is an important issue in the believer's life. (This chapter is derived solely from the booklet by Dr. Kluane Spake, "Understanding Headship.")[1]

I. Understanding Headship *(also mentioned in chapter 2)*

A. Why Study the Word Headship?

1. We study *headship* because the word *"head"* has been erroneously translated to mean having authority over or "being the boss" over the church and home structure. Consequently, our entire Western culture, and most all of Christianity, have been incorrectly influenced into operating according to a chain-of-command patriarchal-supremacy system. The mistranslation of *head* changes the meaning of many Scriptures.

2. We study *headship* because the church must come into unity – and, we're not in unity now.

3. We study *headship* because of the escalating divorce rate among Christians. Great strides have recently been made to enable women in ministry, but still most Christian homes suffer from terribly unbiblical expectations. Women are coerced into deferring to husbands in their home setting, regardless of their apparent capacities and aptitudes. At the same time, men who think they have to make all the decisions and be the "priest of his home" become co-victims of this rigid, incorrect stereotype.

   - Questioning the meaning of *head(ship)*, does not side with rebellion and lawlessness… It doesn't mean that our homes and churches will become places of rivalry, or filled with contention over who's in charge. Marriage is not an earthly relationship or business that needs a boss. It's two people wanting to become one.

- Questioning the meaning of *head(ship)* does not mean that churches are to function without oversight. Scripture distinctly differentiates between the essential need for governmental authority in a church and proper relationships with a family unit. God gives churches governmental authority to rule and assist believers in achieving their potential, both through correction and encouragement. Governmental Scriptures concerning ministerial oversight do not concern the word "head."

B. Genesis (ORIGIN) Contains the Seedbed of Biblical Truth

It all starts in the book of Genesis. That word *genesis* means "the beginning, the ORIGIN and SOURCE of life. Of course we do not receive all our answers from Genesis, but we do find the outline for where humanity came from and the beginning of the Hebrew race and, since that time, everyone has wanted to know the origin of things.

- The Garden became the birthplace of the whole human race! All creation and all nations began in the garden. Eternal principles such as seedtime and harvest have their origin there. Civilization emerged on the sixth day when Adam was made in the image and likeness of God – being ONE person – both male and female. Both genders reflect the image of God.

- Because we usually imagine Adam as being a *male* person, we consider his Maker, the Creator God, as more masculine than feminine. Consequently, most people think of the man more nlearly like God than the woman. But, God is a Spirit that surpasses gender.

- Genesis tells us that both the man and the woman were created equally in the image of God. God said, "*Let us make man* (the term man is universal, not gender specific – i.e., humankind, humanity) *in Our image* (shape, phantom, resemblance) *according to Our likeness* (like fashion, similitude); *and let them* (plural) *have dominion over the fish of the sea....and God called their name Adam"* (Genesis l). Male and female.... This God-like image refers to the faculties that Adam acquired from the Creator to be like Him and to relate to Him. Humanity was made in His image, to be like God.

C. The Five-Fold Commission was given to Adam (being both male and female). The commission means to:
1. Be fruitful – grow, reproduce after one's own kind, to produce again, or bring into existence, to make offspring of its own kind.
2. Multiply – increase, become numerous.
3. Fill the earth – replenish, fill to abundance, to satisfy.
4. Subdue it - conquer, bring under subjection, and tread down.
5. Have dominion – to reign over, take rule over everything that lives other than man.

Adam's primary purpose at creation was to rule over this physical creation and to tend and guard the Garden. There was no striving. In mutuality and equality, Adam (being male and female) had the identical mandate (Genesis 5) to tend and keep (guard and protect) the Garden.

D. Adam was Alone
- God said this condition of aloneness was "not good." The word *"alone"* means separated, only a part, or all in one – The Linear Greek says, "It was not good that Adam's strength was spread out in this way." In other words, there was too much work for one person. This marvelous creature was not able to fulfill the mandate alone, and God said it wasn't good. God created the woman to keep him from being alone.
- She was to be a *helpmeet* (*"ezer,"* which means a superior helper, corresponding counterpart, matching, a face-to-face equal and suitable companion). The Hebrew word *ezer* is never a subordinate word. Fifteen of the nineteen uses of this word refers to God as our *ezer* (helper).

E. Adam was the ORIGIN of the Woman

The woman was drawn <u>from</u> the substance of <u>Adam</u> to share his hopes, his dreams, and his accomplishments. When she was created, Adam saw her and said, *"At last this is bone of my bone and flesh of my flesh."* He recognized his own completion by having a counterpart. They bonded themselves together in covenant as *"one flesh"* both being naked and unashamed.

As two individuals, they still defined God's image and likeness. Together they commanded creation cooperatively and with no job distinctions. This absolute equality was/is the intention of the original creation.

- God separated the woman from the male's side (*tsau-law* (Hebrew) or *pleura* means "side" not "rib," Genesis 2:22). He remained intact.

- She became another entity, a totally separate human person. She was made to be a "helper comparable" *(ezer)* to her mate. God said this new created woman was "very good."

- She was derived from, but not inferior to, Adam. There was no hierarchical arrangement in this relationship. He was not the "set" leader.

- They were now two parts of God's image and likeness. Two separate entities existed, but their instructions did not change.

- Woman was designed to be a co-regent – she ruled with and was not ruled by man. The order of their creation (chronology) had no significance as to their leadership status.

- The mandate of dominion rule didn't change. God did not alter or restrict his command for humans to subdue, conquer, guard, defend and take dominion.

- They were seen as parallel creations. The Creator did not limit her rule over creation. To rule does not cause a woman to lose her femininity, and to not rule jointly breaks the intentional command of creation.

- Submission to another person was not part of God's creative design and God was still the only one in authority.

- Creating woman was to be the final crowning creative act of God for the accomplishment of His purposes.

F. And God Blessed THEM (*Genesis 1:22, 1:28, 5:2*)

1. According to God's original institution of marriage (Genesis 2:24), the man connected (joined) with the woman. Adam knew she was a part of him. He said, *"She is bone of my bone and flesh of my flesh. She shall be called woman because she was taken out of man."* What Adam said is an important statement – that he was

her ORIGIN and SOURCE. ONE person could not do it *"alone."* Because she was *"one flesh"* with him, they could cooperatively fulfill God's mandate, together.

2. What Adam said became the proclamation of the first marriage, COVENANT. Words caused the woman to become a *wife* and Adam to be the *husband.* According to God's original institution of marriage *(Genesis 2:24)* the man connected (joined) with the woman.

3. The marriage formula: one man plus one woman = one flesh. From the dawn of time, God's design was for the man and woman to labor side by side, working and living together in coequal partnership to accomplish the eternal purposes of God. This couple lived as sinless creatures. Their undiminished minds functioned without iniquity. They were both discerning individuals capable of fulfilling the dominion mandate.

4. Since God's original creative intention was for both men and women to rule in corresponding equality, then ultimate redemption will return this divinely-intended standard.

G. The Beguiling One

1. We don't know how long they lived happily in the garden, before the crafty serpent tried to destroy the integrity of the Word of God.

2. One day, he poised himself in the garden. He approached both of them (Adam was there "with her" *Genesis 3:6). Genesis 3* records some of the conversation between them. *"Ye* (plural) *will be like God, Ye* (plural) *will surely not die, your* (plural) *eyes will be opened,"* They questioned the infallible Word of God. They both ate of the wrong tree.

3. Only one command was given *(Genesis 2:16-17),* and that same command was the only one broken *(Genesis 3:11)*. That one command concerned eating and not eating. It had nothing to do with leading.

4. She had been there (as part of Adam) when the first command was given to take five-fold dominion. She knew the instruction to defend and guard the garden. Now as a separated individual, we do not know why she spoke to the serpent, but we do know that he was cunning. I Timothy 2:14 tells us that Eve was deceived (meaning cheated, misled, and deluded). Deceived doesn't mean she lacked intelligence, it

means she was tricked into not ruling over the serpent with dominion. She later responded to the Divine questioning with accuracy, *"The serpent deceived me and I ate"* (vs13).

5. Adam deliberately and willfully defied the divine command. He even told God that it was the woman's fault! Because of his (not her) sin, all of humankind lost out.

   - Jesus died for the sins of Adam,

     "And for this reason He is the Mediator of the new covenant, by means of death, for the redemption of the transgressions under the first covenant, that those who are called may receive the promise of the eternal inheritance." (Hebrews 9:15)

   - All died in Adam, now all live in Christ,

     "For as in Adam all died, even so in Christ all shall be made alive." (I Corinthians 15:22)

H. The Curse Came

1. Because they ate of the wrong tree, two things were cursed:
   - The ground (*Geneses 3:17-19*)
   - *The* Serpent (*Genesis 3:14-15*)

2. God said there would be enmity (a blood war or feud) between the serpent and the woman, and between his offspring and hers.

I. Judgment Came

The people were never cursed, but judgment came. Because of sin, the man was driven from the Paradise Garden and the woman followed (*Genesis 3:23-24*) – both were in a fallen state. In this fallen state, Adam and Eve were the ORIGIN of all humanity.

- After the fall, Adam named his companion Eve or *"mother of* all living."
- They are the only set of parents for all of humankind.
- From these two comes every race, blood type, and nation.
- All of humankind was doomed to die without hope, because of their fallen condition.
- The family structure remained the mainstay of Israel's culture.

J. The Fall Reversed God's Design for Humanity (the following occurred)

- Spiritual death occurred, they lost their immortality with God and physical death came, aging and sickness began. Soul death occurred, their mind, will, and emotions were carnal.
- Their eyes were opened. They knew they were naked (unguarded). They were afraid (1st mention of fear). They knew guilt and shame (1st mention of shame and guilt).
- They lost the revelation and fellowshipping presence of God. Human nature ruled, not the spiritual nature.
- Sin came on all creation and humankind knew good and evil. Self-effort and self-interest became the focus. This is where subordination and patriarchy began.
- Inequality, pain in childbirth, and toiling to grow food all began.

K. The ORIGIN of Submission came after the Fall
- In the garden, there was no decree given to women to submit or be subordinate in any way to the man. But as a consequence of the fall, (*Genesis 3:16*) God says that her <u>desire</u> will be turned to her husband and he shall rule over her.
- This word <u>desire</u> (*tesuqa*) means *turning and leaving*. This verse implies a pre-known observation, a Divine prophetic foresight; God tells Eve what would happen as a result of her voluntarily leaving the garden to be with the man. What happened? Patriarchy and contending domination! This subordination was never part of God's original plan.

From the list above, we see tremendous loss from the deep purposes of God's original plan. Now, we have a theological choice. Either we embrace the entire list of losses as God's present design for today's church, or we must view each loss as a consequence of our fallen condition – the enemy of our inheritance. Inequality is part of the fallen process. How wrong it is for Christians to promote any part of sin and its consequences when Jesus gave his life to conquer it.

L. The Argument

Somehow a woman has an independent free will to be saved, but after the Fall many believe she needs a male overseer or boss to rule and help her. But one must wonder, if no other mediator except Christ exists, then how can we justify the man (or husband) coming between the woman and God? When one person, any person, dominates another – it displaces the divine Lordship of Christ. After all, each person possesses the free will options to choose life or death – blessings or cursing.

M. Jesus Died to Restore Us to the Original Creation Design

Jesus brought redemption, which reverses the results of the fall, into every area of our lives. He was the first-fruit example of how to live in dominion and authority. His sinless life shows us our potential.

- Jesus had women disciples. He touched them, spoke to them in public, and had close friendship with them. He released them into ministry. He never spoke of submission to another person.

- When we were born again, Jesus rejoiced in our conversion. Gender didn't matter. Race and class didn't affect our calling Him "Lord." The only thing necessary for redemption was faith and repentance.

- Redemption is what takes Christianity out of the realms of religion and philosophy and makes it a living reality. Redemption means to restore, to "buy back," or to put back the way it was before. We need the character strength and resolve to access our redemptive promises.

- *Galatians 3:26-29* tells us now that Christ has come, those who are "in Christ Jesus" are sons (both genders) of God by virtue of their faith alone.

    "For you are all sons of God, through faith in Christ Jesus. For as many of you as were baptized into Christ have put on Christ. There is neither Jew nor Greek, there is neither slave nor free, there is neither male nor female; for you are all one in Christ Jesus. And if you are Christ's, you are Abraham's seed and heirs according to the promise."

Whatever inferior positions people may have had in society, all have been abolished in Christ. This declaration of the new creation order gives no hint of further dependency or submissions requirements.

- We are predestinated to conform to the image of Jesus and we become His representatives in action. (*Romans 8:28-30*)

- Embracing the total work of the cross brings us back to Edenic privileges. The word "Eden" means "God's delight." Redemption enables humankind (the New Creation) to return to this spiritual "Image of God."

N. Restoration

- Jesus is held in the heavenlies until the restoration of all things.

    "Whom heaven must receive until the times of restoration of all things, which God has spoken by the mouth of all His holy prophets since the world began." (Acts 3:21, NKJ)

    The completed reality of God's intentions will be accomplished. Restored believes (both men and women) will live with the capacity to execute dominion rule on earth.

- God, from the beginning, set out to authorize his decreed eternal plan for kingdom co-regency on this earth. We (the body corporate) are a kingdom of priests *(I Peter 2:4-5)*. The unanimous priesthood of believers demonstrates equality. Equality and oneness are major purposes in the heart of God.

- The ceaseless stream of God's perpetual design flows from the dawn of humanity until our day. God clearly authorized and decreed His precise eternal plan – that of effective kingdom ministry dynamically impacting the world. This truth is clarified as we overlay Adam's pre-fall five-fold ministry commission over the five-fold ministry in operation. In doing this, we obtain further clarity with extended definition of the five-fold ministry for today.

    1. <u>Fruitfulness</u> – Apostles bring forth others of the same kind. This ministry brings into existence the reproduction and replication of God's likeness and image. (The husbandman patiently waits for fruit, *James 5:7* – the produce of the tree of life.)

    2. <u>Multiplication</u> – The act of increase is predicated upon the prophetic ministry calling into being.

    3. <u>Filling the earth</u> – The action of filling the earth with believers is accomplished by the Evangelists.

    4. <u>Subduing</u> – The pastor leads the congregation into conquering the soul realm and bringing carnality and every evil work into subjection.

5. <u>Dominion</u> – The teacher reveals the *rhema* information necessary for the believer to transform the mind and accomplish dominion.

God's people, originally created to fully function in five-fold ministry, now become restored to "God's delight."

II. What Happened?

A. Historical Facts

The facts prove that women were not barred from church authority until 300 BC. Women did lead in the early church. Archeological evidence and historical documents clearly show that women were: Bishops, priests, apostles, and deacons. Several women headed up churches, built churches, served communion, and taught men. *(Romans 16:1-3, Acts 18:24-26, Philippians 4:2-3, I Timothy 3:11; 5:14 & 17 rule and manage the same word). Women prophesied in church (I Corinthians 11:5; Acts 21:9)*.

There are only a few of many women who led in the Bible.

- Deborah was selected by God *(Acts 13:20)* as ruler, leader, judge, and true prophet of Israel *(Judges 4:4)*, and she officiated over the court. She ruled over males, elders, generals, tribal heads, and all of the children of Israel *(Judges 4:5)*. Barak waited for her orders and obeyed them *(Judges 4:14)*. Her ministry was public.

- Mary Magdalene functioned as the first apostle "sent" by the risen Lord to the original apostles. *(Matthew 28:1-10)*

- The Samaritan women preached to the city. *(John 4:39)*

- Phoebe was a deacon. *(Romans 16:1-2)* She also was called *prostatis* (guardian or protector).

- Junia was of *"note among the apostles."* *(Acts 26:7)* The Elect lady and other women had house churches.

- Priscilla and Aquila went to the synagogue and taught together. *(Acts 18:1-3; 26 & Romans 16:3)*

Redemption totally empowered all people – including women.

B. Women were considered inferior in Greek Culture

Paul wrote to Greek Churches about Greek problems. Greek thought influenced the whole known world. Paul wrote to them about their excesses, restrictions, and their cultural issues.

1. Greeks worshipped a *"secret"* religion of special wisdom. Gnostics believed that Eve was a Celestial power source. They deified certain women and believed in Great Mother Goddess(es) and that humanity had its *"origin"* from a woman. This Great Mother had many names: *Nu Dwa, Aruru, Danu, Sussistanako, Ma, Bellona, Cybele, Demeter, Artemis, Ama Tu An Ki, Maha Devi, and Isis* were only some of the other mythological giant women worshipped. (Earliest archeological evidence shows that Europe, Asia Minor, and Northern Africa also worshiped the Great Mother.) Mother Earth was the *"source"* of all life and crops – and not Almighty Father God.

2. Greek men always kept their social activity separate from their home life. Their wives were kept veiled and cloistered. They never ate or slept with their wives. They didn't have any form of conversation with them. Men spent most of their time away from home, only interacting with them to have children. They had additional relationships for intellectual companionship and sex.

C. Paul's Ministry was to the Greeks

Paul (the apostle to the Greek Gentiles), sought to address these cultural, Gnostic, and mythological issues by teaching that neither the man nor the woman was independent of the other. He asserted that she was a special creation designed to meet all of a man's needs in partnership.

- Paul emphasized the dependence of all humans to the natural birth process *(I Corinthians 11-3; verses 8-12)*. He addresses the interdependence of both genders – the woman being as dependent on the man for her origin as the man is on the woman.

- Paul encouraged men and women to discuss things of God together *(I Corinthians 14:35)*. He gives full equality of sexual rights *(I Corinthians 7:3-5)*

- Paul spoke of Priscilla, Mary, Persis, Thyhaena, Tryphosa, Euodia, and Syntyche as being "yokefellows," also translated "faithful servant," or "co-laborer" with him in the gospel *(Philippians 4:2-3, & Romans 16:1-2)*. (This is the same term also used in *(I Corinthians 3:9; II Corinthians 6:1 & 8:23; Philippians 2:25; Colossians 4:11; I Thessalonians 3:2; Philemon 1:24).*

- Paul emphasized the necessity of order in church services. He refuted Gnostic errors about the Mother Goddess and the prevalent theory that man emerged first from a woman. He also addresses the Greek's devotion to a *"secret mystery"* religion and then tells them the true *"mystery"* *(Ephesians 1:9, 3:3-4 verse 9, 5:32, 6:9; Colossians 1:26-27, 2:2, 4-3; I Timothy 3:9 verse 16).*

D. What the word *"Head"* did NOT Mean

1. Paul often used the Greek word *"keyhale,"* which was translated to mean *"head"* or one in charge. We find that the Hebrew (Old Testament) word for *"head"* is *"rosh,"* which does mean, first in order, captain, chief and ruler. But the New Testament word for *"head"* has a different meaning.

    a. The Greek work *"keyhale"* (which we now translate *"head"*), does not, and never has communicated the meaning of "chief, supremacy, nor boss." *Keyhale*, also never meant decision-maker, superior rank, or final authority.

    b. For centuries, the church has taught that man is the head of the woman – meaning "in leadership over her." We must not continue to assign false connotations to the word, *keyhale*, just because we've been mistaken for such a long time. Examination of other concurrent Greek literature confirms the fact that *keyhale* was not understood to mean "leader or boss."

- The Septuagint translators took great pains to not translate *keyhale* as "one in charge."
- Chrysostom, an early and highly influential Greek Church Father, wrote, "Anyone was a heretic who proclaimed that *keyhale* denoted superior power or authority."
- Coexisting Greek literature and legal documents never used *keyhale to mean* "in charge".

2. The meaning of *keyhale* must be discerned by how the Greeks understood it at the time Paul wrote the letters. If Paul had meant to talk about the head (meaning skull area of the body), boss, or leader, then he knew several other appropriate Greek words – but none of them *keyhale*. The Greek language has different words that do mean topmost

bodily member (*Ephesians 1:22-23*), interdependent with the body (*I Corinthians 12:21; Ephesians 5:23-30*), and the part usually born first (*Colossians 1:15-18*).

3. In the seven passages where Paul used the word *keyhale*, he addressed Greek-speaking converts. If Paul had wanted to express the quality of leadership or ruling, he would have used the word <u>archon</u>, as he did several times *(Romans 13:3)*. He also knew how to use the word <u>exousia</u> to express authority, as he did in *(Romans 13:1-2)*.

- He could have used <u>prostatus</u> to describe an overseer or ruler as he did in *(I Timothy 3:4)*. The <u>prostatus</u> was governmental authority developed for church leadership and order, but not for relationships between husband and wife or men and women.
- *Keyhale* is never intended to mean chief, leader, authority, boss, or the one in charge.

E. What the word *Keyhale* DID mean.

Keyhale was a commonly used buzzword meaning *origin* or *source*. It also meant originator, completed, derivation, enabler, and source of life. This meaning was clear to the first century reader, because they passionately looked for the *origin* or *source* of things.

- Greek was Paul's native tongue. As a brilliant scholar, Paul deliberately chose to use *keyhale* in order to communicate the meaning he had in mind of derivation, *origin* or *source*.
- The true meaning of *keyhale* gives us a more exalted picture of Christ than ever before

F. Why did they translate *keyhale* incorrectly?

Greek was the common language used in many countries at the time the Gospels were written. But eventually, the Scriptures needed to be translated into other languages, and was done so many times. Often the new translations used older ones to help establish meanings and context. The earliest translators had some misunderstandings about what some of the words meant.

1. The first reason for confused translation comes from the understanding of anatomy in ancient times. From Greek teachings, most Bible translators believed that sperm (the source of life) originated in the head (skull). Therefore, what flowed out from

the head represented the origin of things. Greeks and Romans often erected statues of men's heads at the formation (origin) of rivers.

- They even believed that the *"source"* of intelligence came from the heart. (That's why the word *"heart"* referred to in Scripture refers to the mind, will, and emotions.)
- Greeks thought that the liver was the central organ of the vascular system. They didn't realize that the blood circulated through the body, but thought blood formed flesh.

2. These Bible translators made assumptions and mistakes, because of their personal preconceived superstitious fears about their own sexuality. They developed rules of chastity, because women seemed to be the cause for their forbidden sexual desires.

3. Many translators and Church fathers were Greek and they were greatly influenced by Gnosticism that revered the Great Mother Goddess (Eve, Artemis, Cybele, etc.) who created everything.

4. Men who translated the Scriptures assumed that males were dominant. They interpreted the Bible from their understandings. So there was no feminine perspective included then. (For example *anthros* was translated as *"man"* rather than *"human beings."*)

5. In old English grammar, the *source* of something was often said to be from the head of something else (as we say in English, *"the head-waters of a river."*)

G. Prohibitions Happened Because of Mistranslations

Third century church records show a much different attitude than those of previous years. Female restrictions increased as the church became more Eucharistic in nature.

These early Church Fathers were desperately trying to maintain a structure of what they considered legitimate and correct. But even though many of their thoughts were wonderfully inspired, many were not. That's what we challenge – the incorrect restraints of ancient civilization and the inequities of religious tradition such as that which follows:

- The Gnostic Church Fathers such as Irenaeus, Clement, Origen, and Cyprian, decided that sole priesthood authority belonged to the bishop, who alone had the *"keys"* (of Peter).

- This concept of Apostolic Succession and Apostolic authority denied the truth of the priesthood of all believers.

This powerful process of Apostolic Succession assured the continuity of tradition by passing the hierarchical structure of rule from the one leading male priest (who acted in the "person of Christ") to the next ruling priest – only upon death. This essential feature marked the Orthodox Fathers; loyalty to received tradition, which included the appointment of the successive ruling priests. Total male church leadership meant no female input.

1. Apostolic authority insisted that only they were inspired enough to interpret the Scriptures. They separated clergy from laity, reinforced the papal power, lessened the laity rights, repressed women, limited the gifts of the Spirit, and promoted celibacy.

2. Apostolic Fathers decided that only the most *"superior"* clergyman could access the Holy Spirit or mediate with God. That meant that the Spiritual Gifts – once distributed to every believer – were now assigned to the previous era and no longer were to be used by non-clerical people. Simultaneously, both the leadership of women and laymen was completely curtailed and the Gifts of the Holy Spirit were quenched.

3. Apostolic tradition forbade widows to speak to others. If a woman walked downtown (roamed about in public), it could only mean she sought to seduce men. Good widows stayed home day and night praying, and were not defiled by the outside world. Good Christian women were never supposed to wear makeup, fine fabrics, or designer sandals. The major meaning of chastity concerned the *"how and when"* a woman appeared in public.

Beginning about 350 AD, restrictive prohibitions were issued against women:

- The Council of Laodicea forbade women serving as priests or presiding over churches –or approaching the altar.
- The Fourth Synod of Carthage forbade women from teaching men or baptizing.
- The First Council of Orange and the Councils of Nimes, Epaons, and Orleans denied the further ordination of deaconesses.

These and many other restrictions indicate that women previously practiced these positions.

H. Canon Law was Considered Unchangeable

1. Cannon law shaped public policy for centuries. It mandated most matters of a civil nature, all property transactions, probates, and all civil cases concerning clergy. The law of the Church became the power of jurisdiction over all persons that belonged to the Church.

- Law ruled sacraments, civil order, matrimony, and the Eucharist.
- The Priests possessed the only ordained sanction to distribute the sacraments and to pronounce absolution.

2. In 1971, when women asked why they could not hold the Catholic priesthood, the reply was that Canon Law would not permit it. They referred to the 2,414 laws of code; 1,927 concerned decrees and legislation that mandated the roles of women. The effect of these laws eventually filtered into nearly every denomination. This theology states:

The reason for denying women the right to teach is the reason that is absolute and universal, based on the natural condition of inferiority and subjection, that is the position of women.

Fortunately, God gives gifts as "He Wills" to both men and women (Galatians 1:1; II Corinthians 1:1, I Timothy 1:1; Romans 1:1). Ephesians 4:7, 8, 11 tells us that God gives the gifts to all believers, not just selected elite believers. He operates in men and women, clergy and non-clergy.

I. Continued Mistreatment

1. During the European Middle Ages, the Law of Chastisement stated that husbands had the obligation to beat their wives with a stick "out of concern for her soul." Women were considered "empty things" and were sequestered at home for childbearing and hard work.

2. Western Civilization was greatly influenced by these ideas.

- By the 1800's in America, women still had no legal existence apart from the husband. She could not sue, because she didn't exist.
- In 1860, the Stuart Mill Act stated that no legal slaves were allowed, except the mistress of every household.

- By 1910, eleven states still did not permit legal divorce for wife beating.

3. Throughout history, men have thought that they were leaders, and have dismissed women as being less than human in nature. Unknowingly, many men are still co-victims of this rigid stereotype; mistakenly believing that they should make all final decisions, because they are the priest of the home. The Word of God has nothing to say about the man being the priest of his home, or the head of the house. Redemption makes both the man and the woman priests.

III. The Truth of Headship

If we really believe in the absolute validity of the Word of God, we must move from our preconceived ideas to those of Godly accuracy, translating the inspired Greek text faithfully. Earlier, we established that *keyhale* means ORIGIN/SOURCE. It is of particular interest to examine some of the prepositions of the Greek language. The primary preposition "ek" (Strong's #1537) also denotes ORIGIN (the point where action or motion proceeds), from out (of place, time, or cause; literal or figurative; direct or remote). "EK" means "out of, from, by, away from," and reveals the principles of ORIGIN (SOURCE) or CHARACTER.

A. Understanding Paul's Uses of the Word *"Keynale"* – The research evidence is overwhelming that to the early Greek, *keyhale* meant ORIGIN or SOURCE. With this translation, let us examine the following Pauline Scriptures:

1. The context of I Corinthians 11 concerns how men and women should pray and prophesy in public church meetings. The instructions relate to disorderly custom, dress, veiling, wrong teaching, and lifestyle in Corinth. Paul rebukes these Corinthian believers and says that they *"...came together not for better, but for the worse" (verse 17)*. They had legalistic division and needless customs. They failed to maintain church discipline. Here is part of the correction:

2. (I Corinthians 11:3) *"But I want you to know that the head of every man is Christ, the head of the woman is the man, and the head of Christ is God."* Because they misunderstood *head* to mean *boss*, the modern traditionalists used this Scripture as evidence for a chain of command. This Scripture doesn't mean that the Father is ranked

first, with Jesus coming in a big second, then the Holy Spirit follows in importance, coming next is the man, and then the woman.

The Father isn't the *boss* or leader of the Son; the Son isn't the *boss* of the Holy Spirit. They all equally, individually, and all together constitute God. Together they compromise the monotheistic God, in the plurality of three manifest eternal substances as One. The Father is God, the Son is absolute deity, and the Spirit is also divine. Jointly, the Godhead has always existed and are co-equal and co-eternal. The Godhead operates as altogether sovereign, absolute, perfect, omnipresent, omniscient, omnipotent, and immutable.

To understand this Scripture, let's look at the last part first. The *head* (SOURCE, ORIGIN) of Christ is God. This means that Christ came from God. As you know, God subsists as three Persons in One. The union and oneness of the Trinity must remain intact as we properly define this word *head* (*keyhale*) as "originator or completer." Jesus "came forth" as the issue from God.

This Scripture says, the *head* (SOURCE) of Christ (*Christos,* Messiah, the anointed one) is God, (*Theos,* the totality of the Triune God). John 8:42 develops this idea when Jesus said, "*...I proceeded and came forth from God.*" From eternity, the Son always existed. Jesus became the Incarnate Son (*Emanuel, God/man*) sent forth "out of" God to accomplish our covenant redemption.

Continuing with I Corinthians 11:3, the *head* (ORIGIN< SOURCE) of every man is God. Again, this means that man the Adam was not created from a woman (refuting the ever-present Gnostic Mother Goddess teachings that woman (*Lillith*) created man). Man has ORIGIN in the Creator.

The third portion of I Corinthians 11:3 continues the same thought of derivation. The *head* (ORIGIN, SOURCE) of every woman is man. As with so many other Scriptures, this text continues to refute the Gnostic Mother Goddess teachings by explaining that woman has her ORIGIN from man. Some translations of this Scripture (I Corinthians 11:3), often inaccurately translate *keyhale* to read, "the husband is supreme over his wife." But if that were correct, if husband really is supreme and his primary function is to lead in the home, it's very strange that no Scripture trains him on how to perform that position of authority. Instead, he's instructed to love her, to honor her, and to give of himself for her.

3. *Keyhale* Scriptures continued

(I Corinthians 11:8) This Scripture expands this thought of ORIGIN, Man was not made from (ek – out of)) woman, but woman from (ek) man. Yes, the first woman "came from" Adam, and was bone of his bone and flesh of his flesh. Paul continues this thought in (I Corinthians 11:12) by saying, *"For as woman was made from man, so man is now born of woman. And all things are from* (ek, derived out of*) God."*

(Colossians 1:18) Paul often used this head/body metaphor to illustrate Christ and the church and the husband and wife. *"He is the head of the body, the church, who is the beginning, the first-born...."* Christ is the ORIGIN of the church (His bride was born out of His side) – all things flow from His supply. As in the first marriage, Adam and the woman who came from his side became "one flesh" because of covenant words. Now, we have a second marriage – with (our confession of faith) the derived church/Bride is covenantly joined together with Jesus as "one flesh"

- The church is not an institution or a religious organization. To God, it is the issue of His corporate presence, the embodiment of Jesus that continues His life and ministry here on earth.
- The Greek word for church is *Ekklesia,* from two words: *"Ek"* Strong's #537 the primary preposition denoting ORIGIN (the point where action or motion proceeds), from, out from, and #2564 *kaleo*; "call" (properly, aloud).
- As with the first bride, God finds this "called out" bride "very good"! She is that *Ezer* – a superior helper, a corresponding counterpart, a suitable companion. Now, we, His "comparable helpmeet," stand face-to-face, being bone of His bone and flesh of His flesh. *(Ephesians 4:2; 1 Corinthians 11:1).*

- Jesus builds His "called out" church upon the rock of revelation *(Matthew 16:18).*

(Colossians 2:19) This Scripture speaks of a fallen believer who was told to hold fast and not get disconnected from the head. He has lost connection with the *head* (*kephale*, ORIGIN & SOURCE – from (*ek*, out of) whom the whole body – grows as God causes it to grow. (*NIV*) (It seems that disconnection caused this person to not be able to grow or receive nourishment from the SOURCE, therefore he was no longer part of the body – no longer part of the "called out ones.")

(Ephesians 4:14-16) Note the similarity to the above text and also the head/body metaphor, *"Then we will no longer be infants....Instead, speaking the truth in love, we will in all things grow up into Him who is the head* (ORIGIN< SOURCE – growing up into His likeness), *that is , Christ* (vs16) *from* (*ek*, out of) *him the whole body....grow and builds itself up in love, as each part does its work"* *(NIV).* This Scripture stresses Christ as the SOURCE and nourishment for growth.

Ephesians 5:21 provides the topic for one of the most misunderstood passages (context vs. 18-23), *"Submit to one another out of reverence for Christ."* The Bible calls for yieldedness (bending) to one another out of reverence for Christ. This command addresses all Christians and includes several categories of believers who are to practice submission. There's a link between these sections with the word "likewise" (in The Message) for each group in chain-like fashion (3:1, 7). The same kind of submission was demanded of all Christians, and this list naturally includes women (vs 22) who are to submit in exactly the same way (not in a different way) – nothing is added.

- The word for submission (*Hupotassomai*) is almost identical in meaning to the Greek word for love, (*Agapao – husbands, love your wives*). Both words involve responsiveness to the needs of the other. Submission can be explained as a voluntary yielding of one's preferences, except when principle is involved. It implies responsibility, or being brought into a sphere of influence. It means to tie together in purpose or to bring into association. It can also mean to add or unite one person with another *(I Corinthians 15:27-28)*

- Godly submission isn't subordination or being under control, but rather expressing and giving love (agape) to bless someone. Bible submission is always contained in the context of mutual submission. We subject ourselves one to another; willingly and not by forced rule. Only God can subject people and expect obedience. Mutual submission is a voluntary giving of oneself and never implies obedience or subordination. It is mutually directed from both husband and wife for the pleasure and blessing of one another.
- While submission is a Godly principle, Paul made it crystal-clear that it was never correct to yield to another person whose conduct or words were incorrect. *(Galatians 2:5-6)*
- Submission is an absolute Biblical TRUTH that extends beyond gender to all Christians *(Ephesians 5:21, I Corinthians 7:3-4, Galatians 5:13, Philippians 2:3, I Peter 5:5-7)*. Submission is volitional with the sole purpose of imaging the nature of Christ. For Christ's sake, we are to follow in His steps as an example *(I Peter 2:20)*. As equals, we are all to be submitted to our SOURCE, Christ Jesus – He alone is the *head* of our family, the head of the house, the head of the church.

Ephesians 5 continues our now familiar head/body analogy: *"For the husband* (literally male person) *is the head* (ORIGIN/SOURCE) *of the woman as Christ is the head* (ORIGIN/SOURCE*) of the church, his body.* Paul then summarizes by returning to his favorite metaphor, *For the man is the head* (origin/source) *of the woman as Christ is the head* (ORIGIN/SOURCE) *of the church, his body.* Paul compares these relationships and defines their similarity in derivation rather than authority structure or hierarchy.

I Corinthians 12:22-27 gives the example of this desired relationship; *Christ loved the church and gave Himself up for her* (*Ephesians 5:25*). Christ is the Enabler, the One who brings all things to completion. He sacrificially provides the means for His wife/bride to obtain full potential *(vs. 29)*.
- We see the proceeding theme of that which is equitable and unwavering. The concept of the first Edenic marriage repeats itself; couples become "one flesh"

in marriage, just as believers become the bride – flesh of His flesh and bone of His bone (*Ephesians 5:31*). The bride (helpmeet) is equally yoked, mutually submitted in union and communion. Only Jesus is the source of LIFE for the entirety of all of His church.

- One Jesus plus one united church reflecting the image of God = "one flesh".
- Jesus stands in the midst (being the SOURCE) of the churches (*Revelation 1:13)*; He is the center. He's not the top-most (head & face) body part.

Colossians 2:9 context 2:8-15 again uses *keyhale* as SOURCE, *For in him* (God is in Him, you and I are in Him) *the whole fullness of the Godhead dwells bodily, and you* (plural) *have come to fullness* (satisfaction, completion, fulfillment) *of life in him, who is the head* (SOURCE) *of all rule and authority*. Further meditation upon this verse reveals the phenomenal potential for our union together. Here we see that being "in Christ" brings us fullness of life. He is our life SOURCE – the nourisher and enabler of all rule and authority.

IV. Unity and Oneness

Speaking of marriage, Paul tells the Corinthian congregation that he has godly jealousy over them. His desire is to present them as pure virgins to their one Husband, who is *Christ (II Corinthians 11:2)*. Scholars have long used this following verse (*II Corinthians 11:3*) to substantiate their view that women need oversight and covering.

> "*But I fear, lest somehow, as the serpent deceived Eve by his craftiness, so your minds may be corrupted from the simplicity that is in Christ. (NKJ)*

This Scripture says that the whole congregation is capable of being ensnared with the capacity to sin due to deception.

What keeps us from deception is contained in this thought of keeping our minds from being corrupted from simplicity in Christ. What is the focus? Simplicity? But the word isn't simplicity… it's ONENESS. We must not become corrupted from the ONENESS that's in Christ. Strong's defines the word simplicity (#572 haplotes), which means singleness, ONENESS, and sincerity without self-seeking.

- It also means *folded together, enveloped into a single unit.*
- We individually have greater purpose when united together toward a common goal.

In His final Great High Priestly prayer, Jesus prayed that believers would enter into this same concept of ONENESS. *That they all may be one; as You, Father, are in Me, and I in You, that they also may be one in Us, that the world may believe that You sent Me...that they may be one just as We are one." (John 17:21-22, NKJ)*

The tense of this prayer indicates that ONENESS has already been accomplished – it's already done. Just like our salvation and healing – we just have to walk it out. We can't walk it out while living in hierarchy. Becoming one with each other requires a co-mingling of lives that allows the God-given functional strengths to emerge from each member.

A. There's a Gathering of the People into Oneness

1. Together we are one – bonded, amalgamated, and co-mingled. *"This is the mystery, Christ in you the hope of glory." (Colossians 1:27) "You are the temple of the living God." (I Corinthians 3:16)*

2. Gathering demands a complete turning from where we have been going to a straightforward advance wholly toward Mt. Zion. It's not just wanting to come together. We are talking about re-aligning our thoughts and positioning ourselves into the correct access for gathering together.

- I Corinthians 6:17 Clearly shows we are all one in Him. *"But the person (not gender) who is united to the Lord becomes one spirit with Him...."*

- I Corinthians 12:12-13 States if we are one then we are synergistically joined to the Lord. *"....just as the body is one and yet has many parts, and all the parts being many, are only one body, so it is with Christ. For by one Spirit we were all baptized into one body, and were all made to drink of one Spirit."*

- Galatians 3:27-28 Galatians says that to those who are baptized (emerged, enveloped) in Christ, there is no Jew or Greek, bond or free, male or female. That means that believers (all nationalities, classes, and people) are immersed into Him and now have become ONE with Him.

They have clothed themselves with the ONE *"For as many of you as were baptized into Christ have put on Christ. There is neither Jew nor Greek, there is neither slave nor free, there is neither male nor female; for you are all one in Christ Jesus."*

3. If we are baptized into Christ, then we are incorporated into the believer's covenant community. We become a people who are not restricted to ethnic origins and are not divided because of doctrine *(Colossians 3:11)*. The context of *Galatians* says it so plainly that this Scripture alone ought to settle it. All members of God's family are equal in God's sight. The law is over *(Galatians 3:23-24)*.

B. Unity Means One Flesh

1. If there is equality in gender, race, or class, then there can be true unity *(Galatians 3:26-27)*. We are flesh of His flesh *(Ephesians 4)*.

2. The God in the flesh meets each of us personally *(John 1:14)*. Each time someone is converted, that Word becomes flesh again. Believers become part of Him. If we're "one flesh" with Jesus, then we must realize the necessity of being "one flesh" with each other.

4. The ONE body, ONE spirit, ONE flesh relationship is how we are to be joined in this lifetime. It's for eternity starting today. (Adam knew his wife and she conceived – gave birth.) Our ONENESS allows us to birth the ultimate fulfillment of the five-fold commission of *Genesis 1:27-28* and we reveal the functioning Word. The idea of ONENESS and ONE flesh reveals full redemption. It connects or unifies two into one meaningful and responsible unit.

C. It Is Finished *(John 19:30)*

Jesus came to earth to totally rescue us from our fallen state and to illustrate the relational oneness between God and Humanity. He finished His job. He became the "Tree of Life" for all who will partake of Him.

- The fruit of His tree enacts restorative activity that intentionally challenges the facade of our present systems.

- The failure and desperation of prejudicial Christianity is now jarred into a desperate longing for that "Genesis face" – the power of the original position of creation – one of spiritual potency and relevance.

Enthroned at the right hand of the Father, Jesus has already raised us up together (all races, classes, men and women) and made us sit together in Him (*Ephesians 2:9*). There are no assigned seats at the back of the bus in the kingdom. These are not racial or gender-defined facts, but positional facts that apply to all Christians. We (together) are the posterity whom the Lord has blessed (*Isaiah 61:9*).

The writer of Hebrews insists that in these final days, we pay attention to this instruction, and that we do not *"fail assembling ourselves together," (Hebrews 10:25),* So far, we've done a lot of "getting together." But this truth of assembling surpasses just going to church every week! We should begin to assemble in a manner that fitly joins us with others.

D. Our Full Salvation

God created biological differences between men and women to accommodate the "one flesh" reproduction and bring happiness together. Scientific research shows that basic gender differences are mostly based on socialization, culture, and tradition. When we compare men and women, from various nations, it's clear that certain expected norms of "feminine and masculine" traits are culturally induced.

For one person to have the "final say" (in home or church) denies the total revelation of God's image and erroneously defines the true body of Christ. This fallacy feeds uninformed beliefs from the Tree of Knowledge of Good and Evil. Their fruit is barrenness of character and lack of productivity. On the other hand, the cry for maturity releases full redemption that transitions us from attitudes of servitude to emancipated liberty.

Those with penetrative insight must rightly "discern the body" and understand that the body of Christ (us) has its ORIGIN and SOURCE in Christ. He is our all and all. Let us be the demonstration of Ezekiel's wheel with a wheel – it contained thousands of eyes that moved together under the rule of the Spirit as one in the earth.

The Greek word *keyhale* doesn't indicate authority or hierarchical significance, but means "SOURCE" or "ORIGIN." At last, the engrafted Word draws us together because of the One who is our ORIGIN and SOURCE – Christ Jesus.

Our potential inheritance is to be restored to the original pre-fall likeness and image. Ongoing salvation brings us into activated resurrection LIFE – in this lifetime.

Jesus paid a high price for us to become heirs of His great and precious promises and so that we could "participate in the divine nature" *(I Peter 1:4)*. Let's embrace and enact the absolute quality and oneness that God intended for us to find. It is His Edenic delight.

References:

[1] Spake, Kluane, PhD. *Understanding Headship.* Sword Inc., PO Box 941933, Atlanta, GA 31141, (678) 584-0711

End of Chapter Questions

Chapter 8

1. What is the definition of "headship" according to the Bible?
2. What was the five-fold commission that was given Adam (being both male and female)?
3. When and where did the origin of submission begin?
4. List some historical facts that prove women were not barred from church authority.
5. How did Paul emphasize the necessity of order in church service?
6. Define the following concepts: Apostolic Succession, Apostolic Authority, Apostolic Fathers, Apostolic Tradition.
7. What is the interpretation of "keyhale"? Summarize your thoughts on this subject.

Chapter 9 *Developing Pulpit Ministry Leadership*

Women in ministry who are called to speak in areas such as teaching, preaching, or other public speaking should be trained to develop fundamental skills in preparing their messages on a given subject. If we fail as leaders of women's ministry to do this task, we are setting up potential future leaders for failure in relating Biblical truths to women. A potential leader can have a great anointing, but without the proper training in public speaking they can fail to present the fullness of what the Holy Spirit is directing. The Bible says:

"Study and be eager and do your utmost to present yourself to God approved (tested by trial), a workman who has no cause to be ashamed, correctly analyzing and accurately dividing (rightly handling and skillfully teaching) the Word of Truth." (II Timothy 2:15, Amplified)

The training helps them further develop their teaching gifts.

It is a well-known fact that part of the work of the five-fold ministry of prophet, apostle, pastor, evangelist, and teacher, is to preach or teach the truth of the Bible orally. Since the time of Christ, the majority of believers receive Jesus as Savior, through a powerful public presentation of the Gospel. That is why it is important to train leaders to make a presentation in the strongest possible way.

The spiritual health of believers, after they have accepted Jesus Christ, depends upon the quality of the teaching and preaching they hear. If leaders do this part of His work well, His people will grow in Godliness. The final result will be that the believer is equipped to effectively share the Word of God as an ambassador, a soul winner for Christ. Preaching/teaching can be described as the manifestation of the *"living Word,"* developed from the *"written Word,"* and delivered by the *"spoken Word."*

- Living Word – Jesus Christ is the living Word. Jesus Christ can be seen in the pages of Scripture from Genesis to Revelation.
- Written Word – The Bible is the written Word. The foundation of any Christian message must be based on large portions of the Holy Scripture.
- Spoken Word – A preacher's oral proclamation of the living and written Word.

If a leader invests time studying and applying its principles, allowing the *"living Word"* to become more real, the *"written Word"* to become clearer, and the *"spoken Word"* to become more powerful, the results will be transformed hearers of the word. This section is aimed at helping leaders to accomplish this important goal.

A. Teacher Training[1]

1. <u>Introduction</u> – The Biblical plan of spiritual multiplication is teaching faithful men who are able to teach others.

> *"And the things that you have heard from me among many witnesses, commit these to faithful men who will be able to teach others also."* (II Timothy 2:2, NJK)

If you are to fulfill this plan, you must constantly be training teachers.. Two basic needs for teacher training are discussed in this section and practical steps are given for planning a training program. Guidelines are also given on how to recruit students for training, how to conduct the sessions, and for placing trained teachers in the ministry.

2. <u>Two Basic Training Needs</u> - There are two basic needs for teacher training in the church: pre-service and in-service training.

   a. Pre-Service Training - Pre-service training is training given before a believer begins to serve in the ministry as a teacher. It is a program of study that will help him learn how to teach.

   b. In-Service Training - In-service training is given to those already serving as teachers in the ministry. The training helps them further develop their teaching gift. Jesus provided both types of training for His disciples.

3. <u>Planning a Teacher Training Program</u> - Here are steps for planning a teacher-training program in your ministry.

   a. Enlist the cooperation of the pastor or spiritual leader of the ministry.

   b. Ask people who are already effective teachers to assist as leaders who will teach others.

   c. Meet with these leaders to set:

      1. Objectives for the training program: Determine the needs of current teachers and potential teachers. State the objectives you want to accomplish in the training program.

      2. Dates, times, and place for training.

3. Leaders who will teach in the training program: Who will teach what and when?
4. Entrance requirements for the program: Who will you permit to attend? They must be born-again believers, of course, but you may have other requirements you want to set. (See suggestions in the "Guidelines" section of this chapter).
5. Standards required for completion of the program: What is required of them to complete the training? (For suggestions, see the "Guidelines" section of this chapter).
6. Type of training event. (For suggestions see the "Guidelines" section of this chapter for various types of training events.)
7. Budget [expenses] for teacher training: How much will it cost? Where will the funds come from?
8. Training materials to be used: These requirements can be used to train teachers. You may want to supplement it with training unique to your denomination and/or the curriculum you plan to use.

d. Prepare a calendar for the year and list all training sessions on it. Include the dates, times, and places.
e. Prepare a ministry description for teachers. This will identify the responsibilities of a teacher for those who are considering enlisting in the training
f. Prepare a teacher's pledge for potential teachers to sign. This is a document that identifies the commitment of the teacher. (Again, see the "Guidelines" section of this chapter for a sample pledge).

4. <u>Recruiting for the Training Program</u> – Here are steps for recruiting people for the teacher- training program.
   a. Invite current teachers for in-service training.
   b. Make an announcement regarding the training. Ask potential teachers who are interested to contact you.
   c. Make personal contact with those you know or have observed and whom you believe have the spiritual gift of teaching.

d. Review applicants who are not already teaching to be certain they meet the entrance requirements you have set for the teacher-training program.

e. Notify all who qualify of the date, time and place of the first session.

5. <u>Conducting the Training</u> - Here are some guidelines for conducting teacher-training sessions:

a. Start each session on time.
1. Begin with prayer that the Holy Spirit will anoint the teachers and will open the hearts and minds of students to learn.
2. Take attendance. Students should be required to attend a certain number of class sessions in order to complete the course.
3. Make sure each student has a copy of any written materials concerning the lesson to be taught.

b. Have all necessary supplies on hand to teach the lesson. These might include visual aids, a teaching manual, and similar items.

c. Allow time for questions and answers about the material you have taught in the session.

d. Give assignments for students to complete prior to the next meeting. These might include reading, writing, or teaching assignments.

e. Unless the Holy Spirit moves differently, keep within the time set for the class. Dismiss students on time.

6. <u>Placing Teachers</u> - Teacher training is not effective unless those you train are actually used in a teaching position. Here are some guidelines for placing teachers in the ministry.

a. Consult the Pastor (if your women's ministry is affiliated with a church or consult the various area leaders of your women's ministry). Where do they have need for teachers? Where do they believe an individual would be most effective? They are also responsible for guiding the gifts and talents of those who are part of the church or women's ministry.

b. Place according to call and abilities - Consider the abilities of the person being placed. Will they be effective in the group they are to teach? Has God given them a special call to this particular group? For example, the Apostle Paul was effective with Gentile people because of the call God gave Him and his personal background and abilities.

   c. Place according to age interest - Some people have no interest in teaching teenagers, or older women, for example. All ages need to be taught, but a teacher should have either an interest and/or a call to work with a specific age group.

   d. Allow opportunities for practice teaching. Let the new teacher serve first as a substitute teacher when the regular teacher cannot be present. Then let them teach several lessons with an experienced teacher observing. After the lesson, the observer can privately share helpful suggestions with the new teacher.

7. <u>Teacher evaluation</u> - After a teacher is serving in the women's ministry, their ministry should be evaluated periodically. Jesus did this with His disciples after He sent them out to minister. They reported back all they had said and done *(Mark 6:7 and 30)*. Evaluation helps identify and correct problems in teaching. It gives an opportunity for spiritual leaders of the ministry to assist teachers in further developing their spiritual gift of teaching. Here are some ways to evaluate a teacher:

   a. Have each teacher do a self-evaluation, then review the results with them.

   b. Evaluate on the basis of the ministry description: Are they fulfilling the requirements of the ministry description for their teaching position?

   c. Are they keeping the commitment of the teacher's pledge that they signed?

   d. Observe the teacher actually teaching. Are they effectively communicating God's Word to their peers? What can they do to improve the way they present the material? Share some positive suggestions with them.

   e. Evaluate the "fruit." The Bible says that "fruit" [results of ministry] can be observed *(Luke 6:43- 44)*.

Remember: Evaluation and correction of problems should always be done in a loving and positive way.

<u>GUIDELINES</u> – Additional Information for Teacher Training

The following additional guidelines may be used to plan a teacher-training program:

1. List the objectives of your training program:

2. Schedule the dates, times, and places on a master calendar for the year. (Use a calendar to do this).

3. Establish entrance requirements for the program. An applicant should:
   - Be a born-again believer.
   - Have followed the example of Christ in water baptism.
   - Be Spirit-filled.
   - Attend church services regularly (and/or be a member of the church).
   - Have a good reputation in church and community.
   - Meet Biblical qualifications for leaders.
   - Demonstrate fruit of the Holy Spirit and Christ-like behavior in daily living.

4. Set standards for completion of program. Some suggestions are:

   Applicants must:
   - Attend all training sessions unless excused due to illness or emergency approved by the leader.
   - Complete all class assignments.
   - Practice teach at least one lesson with a leader observing.

5. Determine the type of teacher-training event. Here are some suggestions:
   - Brief training as part of regular teachers' meeting: If the teachers of the ministry meet regularly, use part of each meeting for in-service training.
   - Self-instruction: Give potential teachers a copy of this material and have them complete the lessons in individual study.
   - One-night training: Meet one night a week to train.
   - Series: Meet in a series of meetings for training. For example, Monday through Friday of a certain week.
   - Retreat - Take teachers to a camp or retreat for training.
   - One-on-one - Assign an experienced teacher to train a new teacher on a one-on-one basis.
   - United training - Perhaps several churches in the community may want to plan a united training event where all the teachers of women's ministries come together for fellowship and training.

- Audio-visual training: If you have audio tape or video tape facilities, record the training and let potential teachers study independently.

6. Select the leaders who will teach, what areas they will cover, and when they will teach. Make a chart with the headings of Name, Dates, Subjects.

7. What training materials will you use?

  Name of training course: _____

  Publisher's Name: _____

  Address:_____

8. Prepare a budget:

  What will it cost to advertise the program? $_____

  What will the training materials cost? $_____

  Other expenses: $_____

9. Prepare a ministry description of responsibilities for potential teachers. Here is an example to follow:

MINISTRY DESCRIPTION

Teacher _____

Ministry Title: Teacher.

Ministry Description: The teacher will assume personal responsibility for:

- Preparing for and teaching the weekly class session.
- Day_____Time_____Place_____
- Recruiting new members to join the class.
- Contacting absentee students and inactive members to determine problems, minister, and reinstate as active members.
- Winning unsaved members to the Lord Jesus Christ.
- Ministering to the spiritual needs of class members who are already believers, leading them in spiritual growth and development, equipping them for the work of the ministry.
- Encouraging class members to become an active part of the total fellowship.
- Completing any required church records pertaining to this class, i.e., attendance records, etc.

Personal Requirements:
- Called of God to this specific ministry.
- Meet Biblical leadership qualifications.
- Completion of teacher training course offered by this ministry.
- Ability to communicate effectively.
- Active member of this women's ministry.
- In agreement with the doctrinal position of this women's ministry.
- Supportive and in harmony with leadership.

Time Commitment:
- Personal preparation time for regular class meeting.
- Regular class meeting time: Two hours weekly.
- Monthly staff meeting.
- Annual in-service teacher's training class.
- Time for personal association, fellowship, follow-up, and ministry to students.

10. Prepare a teacher's pledge of commitment. Here is an example to follow:

TEACHER'S COMMITMENT

Having received Jesus Christ as my personal Savior, and now living in fellowship with Him, I realize that ministering Christ and His word to others is a high calling. In view of my commission as a teacher and relying on the help and guidance of the Holy Spirit, I pledge that:

- I agree with the doctrinal statement of (name of ministry), and will teach nothing in conflict with it.
- I will daily set aside time for prayer and Bible study.
- I will earnestly pray for the conversion of my students and for the spiritual growth of those who are Christians.
- I will faithfully spend time preparing each message, and will prepare myself spiritually by living the truths I teach.
- I will be faithful in my teaching position in the (name of ministry).

- I will teach from God's Word, promote study of the Bible by my peers and encourage their active participation in the different sessions.
- I will faithfully attend and promote the services of our (name of ministry), and will support financially and with my prayers.
- I will attend any meetings required, unless hindered by some reason I can conscientiously give to God.
- If for some reason I cannot fulfill my responsibilities, I will consult with my leaders and surrender my duties if that seems advisable.

Name:_____Date:_____

B. How to Prepare and Teach a Message/Sermon

The following section is a proposal to present to beginning leaders or leaders wanting help in the basic preparation of her messages/sermons. It deals with the composition and proclamation (delivery) of the sharing of the Word of God. It is based on teaching notes from Dr. R. Tanon.[2]

1. A "Sermon" is a communication of ideas and information by talking based on Christian doctrine, with the objective to teach divine truth with the end result being to:

    1. Convince the unbelievers.
    2. Strengthen the spiritually weak.
    3. Correct them who may be going astray.
    4. Stimulate the believers into practicing Christian virtues.

The speaker should decide which of the above will be the goal of her sermon before choosing the theme.

2. Composition of Sermons – Principle Components - The sermon should have three principal components: The Introduction, The Body, and The Conclusion.

    a. The Introduction – is the first part, which prepares the hearers for the body of the sermon. It advises hearers on the theme, and wakens interest in it. Therefore, the introduction should be strictly related to the theme. It should not he long, five minutes more or less as a general rule.

b. <u>The Body</u> is the principal part of the sermon. It is here where you present and develop the theme. It is here where you explain and apply the sermon to the needs of the hearers.

c. <u>The Conclusion</u> is the final touch with which you close the sermon. It should be brief and it should appeal directly to the hearers so as to impel them to make a decision.

<u>Note:</u> The principle Components – (the Introduction, the Body, and the Conclusion will be discussed more in depth in Section 6 "The Sermon Body").

The components of an outline should also have the following:[3]

- Color - Interest, drama, impact, curiosity value
- Unity – Each part belonging
- Sequence – Each section flowing naturally into the next
- Balance – No one part having disproportionate space (don't over-emphasize unimportant points)
- Conclusion – The beginning and end should both be planned (the end, in fact, may be more important than the beginning; make it a true climax, not a feeble anti-climax).
- Interesting – The speaker should be attracted to and have interest in, and enthusiasm for the Scripture she has selected.

3. <u>Selection of Material</u>

a. All material should be God-centered exclusively

1. The speaker should adopt an unadulterated Biblical approach *Preach the word! Be ready in season and out of season. Convince, rebuke, exhort, with all longsuffering and teaching (II Timothy 4:2).*

2. The Spiritual relationship of the preacher with God is the main source of inspiration for sermon material.

♦ PRAYER, PRAYER, AND MORE PRAYER
♦ Divine revelations must coincide with the Scriptures
♦ FASTING
♦ Meditation

3. No other stand, political, personal or otherwise can take the place of the WORD. *(I Timothy 6:20, 21, II Timothy 2:16)*

b. Material Source

1. Books

    a. The Bible; MAJOR SOURCE

    b. Other books - Christian literature

    c. General books, magazines, Christian periodicals, etc.

2. People

    a. Varied needs, culture and living styles

    b. Christian sharing - the brethren

3. Nature

    a. God's creation - other scenarios

4. Life experiences of the speaker

    a. Sinner and/or past life

    b. Christian growth

    c. Personal problems

4. <u>The Theme</u> - About what will I speak?

a. The Theme is the Message condensed...and the Message is the Theme developed.

   <u>NOTE</u>: The word "Title" means name, while theme means topic.

   <u>EXAMPLE</u>:

   <u>Title</u>: "The Last Message"

   <u>Theme</u>: "Christ is Coming"

(Titles are used only when you are preaching a series of sermons over a period of time)

b. Principles that govern the Theme choice

1. Be in touch with God - The principal priority is your daily spiritual walk. Anointing, divine revelation, inspiration, all come from your daily Christian living.

2. Be in touch with the Bible - Bible knowledge acquired by a systematic study and daily search of the Scriptures.

3. Be in touch with People - Sensitivity to the needs of the listeners, using a biblical approach to communicate the gospel within their understanding.

c. Guidelines for Theme Selection

1. Seek diversity in your themes
   a. Be mindful of your recent messages
   b. Try not to be locked into one theme or line of thought
   c. Be aware of the wide range of needs: salvation, healing, holiness, deeper life, etc.
   d. Consideration of special occasions is a must (most of the time)
2. The speaker must understand the theme. A clear and precise concept of the material is necessary.
3. The listeners must also understand the theme with little difficulty. <u>Be Careful -- Avoid tricky themes</u>.
4. Your theme choice should be based on doctrines, truths and fundamentals in Holy Scripture. <u>Avoid frivolous or unrelated themes</u>.
5. The theme should be in accordance with the speaker's personal experience or expectation.
6. The theme must adapt to:
   a. Time
   b. Place
   c. Occasion

d. The Classification of Themes

1. Doctrinal - The sermon that presents doctrine; Salvation, the God-Head, etc.
2. Moral Ethics - The sermon that encourages the right principles of conduct; rather than lying, cheating, adultery, etc.
3. Historical - The sermon that involves past events concerning a particular nation, people, field of knowledge or activity, especially concerning a specific group or subject in a chronological order.
   EXAMPLES: Creation, the Jewish Nation, Prophets, etc; with the intention of teaching and applying to the present for spiritual growth.

4. Experiential - Sermons related to the spiritual experience of your listeners for individual growth.

   EXAMPLES: Overcome temptation, Spiritual warfare, etc.

5. Special Occasion - Sermons related to a particular occasion, such as a wedding, funeral or baby dedication, etc.

e. Preliminary Theme Check

   After choosing the theme, answer these four questions in relation to your sermon development:

   1. What do I want to say? - Know clearly and be able to define the truth to be declared.

   2. Why? - Discover the reason and need for your theme.

   3. How? - How can the listener relate and appropriate the sermon to his/her personal life?

   4. What should be done? - Challenge your listeners to put into practice the sermon truth.

   NOTE: Not all of these questions need to be used in every sermon. Choose the appropriate aspects that deal with the particular theme to be presented.

5. <u>The Text</u>

   The word "text" in reference to a sermon means a verse or portion of Scripture used as the "thread" or basis in the development of the principal truths of the theme. Qualities of a good Scripture text should be:

   - Not too difficult - Easy to comprehend and to interpret, both to the leaders and audience, selecting Scripture texts which are not controversial, but easy to interpret and apply.
   - Interesting – The speaker should be attracted to and have interest in, and enthusiasm in the Scripture she has selected.

   a. Gathering a variety of texts

      1. Know your Bible

      a. You should read the Bible daily.

      b. Mark your Bible for message possibility.

      c. Memorize favorite passages, verses.

  b. Guidelines for text selection

    1. The text should be clear

    2. The text should embrace the theme

    3. The text is more than a starting point. It should flow through your sermon. You can refer to it when appropriate.

    4. The text should not be oblique or twisted.

    5. The text should not be of dubious, doubtful interpretation.

    6. Do not use a text to fit a prevailing circumstance. It can be later interpreted or used as mockery.

    7. Do not avoid the verses of the Old Testament.

    8. Well- known passages should not be avoided.

  c. The text in relation to the context

    1. Consider carefully the context.

    2. The context should not overshadow the text.

    3. Occasionally the text has no relation with the context. In such a case, avoid the context.

6. <u>The Sermon Body</u>

After choosing a theme, a text, and material for the sermon, your next step is to arrange the material in an orderly and effective manner.

The speaker is like an architect. Her job is to construct a building with the materials at hand. From the same material she can either build a jail or a palace. The plan or blueprint (outline) indicates the structure.

The coordination of the respective parts of a sermon helps the teacher and audience to understand clearly and retain the sermon truth.

  a. Distinctives of an orderly sermon are:

    1. Has one theme - common error of new speakers - too many themes

2. That the development of the sermon be natural, logical, having view of end results desired. The sermon should appeal to:
   a. Intellect
   b. Emotions - stimulating the will, encouraging a decision to act.
3. It is considered out of order to exhort, scold or warn, before instruction or application of a truth without explanation of such.

b. The Sermon Introduction
   1. The purpose of the introduction
      a. To stimulate interest in the theme
      b. To prepare the congregation for the sermon
   2. Material source for the introduction
      a. Introduce the known by the unknown. Your audience's life experience can be a link to your sermon.
      b. The Text: Sometimes the text provides the best material for your introduction; from text structure, familiarity or misinterpretation.
      c. Historical setting of the text
      d. Geographical relation: Bible dictionary and maps can be of use
      e. The Theme: In relation to the times - special days, climate, wars, national problems, or common dilemmas
      f. Customs: Biblical times or contemporary way of life
      g. Illustrations: An example, comparison, anecdote, etc. by which your theme is explained
   3. Distinctives of a good introduction
      a. Should not be boastful, promising more than you can deliver.
      b. Not too emotional
      c. Do not start with a high-pitched or loud voice.
      d. Should not relate directly with the sermon following.
      e. Should be short and to the point.
      f. Should be well planned and prepared, preferably after the outline is defined. Do not wait until just before sermon delivery.

c. The Body of the Sermon

The body is the main part of the sermon. The body is the presentation and application of the sermon theme. The sermon body is developed by "divisions." The divisions are developed by "sub-divisions."

The major parts of a well organized discourse are distinguished by its "divisions..

1. Advantages of divisions

   a. To the speaker

      1. It keeps her bound to the theme – without a "rightly" divided sermon, a teacher will have difficulty developing her sermon – there will be a tendency to stray from the theme.

      2. It helps with sermon creativity – enfolds chronological progression, encourages progressive thought patterns, facilitates sermon composition.

   b. To the audience

      1. It stimulates interest - a continual flow is easy to follow if divided in logical order.

      2. It serves as a guide for the purpose of the sermon

   c. To the sermon itself

      1. It clarifies and makes for easy understanding.

      2. The non-outlined sermon is aimless and leaves confusion as to what was said. "Sounded good, but I can't remember anything."

      3. Do not add a division unless you have something say about it related to the theme.

2. Necessary ingredients for division preparation

   a. Interesting: Each division should demonstrate singular interest

   b. Clear: There is major value in a clear simple statement rather than a profound indefinite one.

   c. Progressive: A sequence of thoughts, each derived from the theme by a consistent relationship.

d. Symmetry: Uniformity of thought, phrase and style. The arrangement of divisions should be written (as much as possible) in symmetrical harmony.

3. Presentation of divisions

a. They should be easily discerned... the audience should be able to identify your divisions.

b. Verbally declared: The heading of each division should be declared in the sermon in its proper order.

EXAMPLE: "WHERE DO YOU SIT?"

1. Lot sat at the Gate of Sodom
2. Peter sat afar off
3. Lame man sat at the temple entrance
4. Mary sat at the feet of Jesus

4. Progression of the divisions: The divisions should be progressive, enfolding toward the conclusion in a crescendo. Keep in mind the following points:

a. The material gathered by the speaker for each division will determine their importance and/or impact.

b. Consider the least important point and place in order ending with the most important point as a climax. NEGATIVE/POSITIVE.

c. Consider the needs and feelings of the audience. Be tactful when presenting a sermon or divisions that deal with sensitive areas. "The Word" is the most appropriate source of material.

Remember that "The Word" is a sword, the Holy Spirit is the soothing oil over hurt wounds. "BE SENSITIVE."

d. The historical order - When presenting a past event, follow a chronological order, etc.

5. Number of divisions

a. Avoid using the same pattern for every message. It will become monotonous and lack spontaneity.

b. As a general rule, use at least two divisions, but no more than five.

6. Derivatives of the divisions
   a. Direct from the words of the text - Textual
   b. Suggested from the text - Topical - either from the context, or ideas created by the preacher (inspired)
7. The use of sub-divisions

   Follows and explains the division. It provides the meat or filler that completes the thought necessary to enhance the message.

   a. Presentation of sub-divisions
      1. Do not announce or declare them as sub-divisions. Only the main divisions are announced.
      2. Try to avoid going beyond this level of division/subdivision making for outline use:

   EXAMPLE: I.
         A.
              1.
                 a. (only if absolutely necessary)

   b. Quality of sub-divisions
      1. Unified - They present the essential parts of the division. Do not place material pertaining to one division in another division.
      2. Wholeness- Make sure to "link" the sub-division with the main division, making complete the union; One thought, argument, or whole presentation.
      3. Order - The sub-divisions present in order all the essential parts of the main division.

7. <u>The Conclusion of the Sermon</u> - should not take more than five minutes.
   PREPARE THE CONCLUSION WITH MUCH CARE.
   a. Four methods to conclude the sermon:
      1. Recapitulation: To review "briefly" or sum up the main divisions of the sermon. Avoid the tendency to re-preach the sermon.

2. Illustration: To explain or make clear by means of an example story, etc.
3. Application: The act of applying your sermon as a remedial agent to the need of your audience.
4. Appeal: An earnest supplication to awaken a favorable response to the sermon's teaching. (Not to be confused with the altar call.)

b. Precautions for the conclusion

1. Learn to STOP. Do not continue to speak after the conclusion. Emotions can get carried away...Let Go - Let God...
2. After saying you are going to conclude, do so. "In conclusion;" "Now to end my sermon;" "My last thought is.."
3. Make a "safe" landing - meaning, not to end abruptly.
4. The conclusion and the altar call are separate. Don't confuse.
5. The conclusion precedes the altar call at all times.

8. <u>The Classification of Sermons – Textual, Topical and Expository</u>

a. Textual: It is based on one or more texts and the divisions are solely from the text. A study of the grammatical phrases offers the divisions for the text.

The textual sermon bases the body of the sermon from words, phrases, or sentences from the text.

b. Topical Sermon: A sermon based on the theme and the divisions created by the speaker's own mind, with the leading of the Holy Spirit.

c. Expository Sermon: A sermon expounding facts from a large portion of Scripture in a detailed manner. The divisions are extracted from the passage of Scripture itself.

9. <u>The Use of Illustrations</u>

To explain or make clear the message by use of examples, comparisons, anecdotes objects, etc., we use illustrations.

The windows of conversation are the illustration. They bring light to what is communicated for better comprehension.

Jesus used illustrations such as: sheep, wolves, camels, and other animals. Vines, pearls, gold, salt, etc. He made very clear His profound spiritual truths with illustrations, (and parables,) from nature and the life experiences of His audience.

a. Material source for illustrations

1. The Scriptures
2. Newspapers - World news (and local), Radio/TV
3. Books, religious history, biographies
4. Poems and other literature
5. From life - Nature, culture, family, etc.
6. Art, posters, just about anywhere you may find an illustration.

b. Advice and Guidelines for use of illustrations

1. Simplicity makes for clarity
2. Must make clear the point you are trying to teach/preach.
3. An illustration is not a division, nor should you make a division to fit an illustration.
4. Do not exaggerate or lie to improve impact, especially if you are using someone else's experience as if it were your own.
5. Be mindful not to use too many illustrations in a sermon (overkill) or you will end up with a house with only windows.
6. If your illustration involves you or your family, you may, if you care to, use the third person in dialogue. Be careful not to become too personal so as to embarrass your loved ones. BE SENSITIVE.
7. Know the following for illustration use:
    a. Must be clearly presented. If the illustration is not clear to the speaker, it will not be clear to the hearer.
    b. Should stimulate the feelings (senses). If the illustration does not move, touch, or stimulate the speaker, it will not move the hearer.
    c. Must be dominated. Review well your illustration so that you may repeat it in the pulpit without mistakes.

d. Should produce: The illustration that is meaningless and has no direction is useless. An illustration should produce an impact on the hearers, should "bear fruit, bring into focus" the theme.

<u>A SERMON IS SOUGHT IN PRAYER, TAUGHT THROUGH PRAYER, AND BROUGHT TO A DECISION IN PRAYER.</u>

C. Altar Call

The Purpose: To summon, to convoke, convene, to produce a reaction and elicit a commitment before the presence of God. Give the audience an opportunity to make a decision, one way or another, either to accept the message preached or reject it.

Generally, an altar call is made after the sermon's conclusion.

1. <u>Who makes the altar call?</u>

   a. The leader - preferred, most effective

      1. She is the person most aware of her aim and the action/reaction she feels she wants to lead her audience into.
      2. She is into the Spirit of the sermon, and has the anointing

   b. Leader of the women's ministry - can be effective

      1. Some leaders insist on making the altar call
      2. Yet, she may not be in the Spirit of the sermon
      3. Many times she is called out of the service because of a problem, etc.
      4. If the leader is not careful, some hazards may occur.
      5. If you are the leader and have a guest speaker, be attentive to the sermon and be ready (prepared) to make an altar call if asked. Be tuned in and in the Spirit. Be prayerful, asking God to give you the same Spirit as the speaker has.

2. <u>Guidelines for the Altar Call</u>

   a. Make known to the host speaker your intention before the service. You may want to discuss your reason or aim with her.
   b. Not all sermons and/or services lead to an altar call.

    c. Consider time, place, culture, and denominational background of the congregation.

    d. The altar call should put into action your sermon truth.

    e. Be ready to minister in a personal manner
        1. To individuals: various age groups and needs
        2. Take time to pray. DO NOT RUN OFF.

Developing an effective pulpit leadership should be an important part of developing women in fulfilling their destiny and furthering your women's ministry.

References:

[1] Pat Hulsey, Ph.D. *Teaching Tactics.* Harvestime International Institute

[2] Dr. R. Tanon (2000). *Teaching Notes: Dynamics of Teaching the Word,* Vision International College & University

[3] Ken Chant, Th.D (1995). *The Pentecostal Pulpit.* Vision Publishing.

End of Chapter Questions
Chapter 9

1. Define the differences between the "living word," "written word," and "spoken word."
2. What are the two basic training needs for serving as teachers in ministry?
3. What are the steps the text refers to in recruiting people for a teacher's training program?
4. How should a trained teacher prepare to teach a message/sermon?
5. What are the components of a sermon and how would you summarize each component?
6. What are the classifications of themes?
7. What are the guidelines for an altar call?
8. Summarize any thoughts you may have, (pro or con) about the material in this chapter.

PART IV

EVANGELISM/OUTREACHES

"But when He saw the multitudes, He was moved with compassion for them, because they were weary and scattered, like sheep having no shepherd. Then He said to His disciples, 'The harvest truly is plentiful, but the laborers are few, therefore pray the Lord of the harvest to send out laborers into His harvest.'"

(Matthew 9:36-38, NKJ)

PART IV: Evangelism/Outreaches

In order for evangelism to occur effectively, the first step is to become a witness for Christ regarding His life-changing effect on our lives and to do what He told us to do in scripture.

> *(Mark 15:16, Amplified) "He said to them, Go into all the world and preach and publish openly the good news (the Gospel) to every creature (of the whole human race)."*

God always blesses and brings many souls into the Kingdom of God as we obediently declare the "good news,"

The second step is for new believers is to be rooted and grounded in love and faith through a discipled life in Christ.

> *(Ephesians 3:17-19, Amplified) "May Christ through your faith (actually) dwell (settle down, abide, make His permanent home) in your hearts. May you be rooted deep in love and founded securely on love. That you may have the power and be strong to apprehend and grasp with all the saints (God's devoted people, the experience of that love) what is the breadth and length and height and depth (of it); (that you may really come) to know (practically, through experience for yourselves) the love of Christ, which far surpasses mere knowledge (without experience); that you may be filled (through all your being) unto all the fullness of God (may have the richest measure of the divine Presence, and become a body wholly filled and flooded with God Himself),*

This will enable the new disciple of Christ to be able to evangelize effectively.

The third step comes through the process of equipping the saints for the work of the ministry.

> *(Ephesians 4:12, NKJ) "For the equipping of the saints for the work of ministry, for the edifying of the body of Christ."*

The work of training and mentoring them (women-to-women) with the goal of producing "harvest gatherers" is key. The end products are "leaders" who will continue the same process with other women. Part III, "Training, Discipling, and Developing Leadership" addressed the process of developing women to become "harvest gatherers."

In evangelizing through outreaches, there has never been a time in history where women have been used more effectively. There are many mission fields to be explored and God is mobilizing 21st Century women to be a force that the devil must reckon with. In today's mission's strategies of women believers, the focus is positive, anointed, and bold, and, because of its reliance on Christ, can help take the world by storm, producing a successful harvest in the Kingdom of God.

In the following chapters we look at some of these outreaches, such as:

- Women's Community Outreaches
- Conference & Retreat Outreaches
- Prison Ministry & Re-Entry Outreaches

In each one of these outreaches (if your ministry decides to promote them), hopefully, there will be a "spiritual wakening," not only for the participants but for the leaders. Most leaders will agree that the blessing they receive from evangelizing is sometimes even greater than the end results of souls being won to the Kingdom. Many outreaches that have swept the world began with a sovereign move of God as they begin praying and waiting on the Lord for His divine purpose.

Christ advised us to count the cost before we begin. This is a wise teaching. It takes tremendous commitment, time and energy to develop an outreach.

(Luke 14:28-33) "For which of you wishing to build a farm building, does not first sit down and calculate the cost (to see) whether he has sufficient means to finish it? Otherwise, when he has laid the foundation and is unable to complete (the building), all who see it will begin to mock and jeer at him. Saying, 'This man began to build and was not able (worth enough) to finish.' Or what king, going out to engage in conflict with another king, will not first sit down and consider and take counsel whether he is able with ten thousand (men) to meet him who comes against him with twenty thousand? And if he cannot (do so), when the other king is still a great way off, he sends an envoy and asks the terms of peace. So then, any of you who does not forsake (renounce, surrender claim to, give up, say good-bye to) all that he has, cannot be My disciple."

We can accomplish the task, if we put our trust in God to complete the work He has begun in His ministry.

Chapter 10 *Women's Community Outreaches*

The essence of women's community outreaches is that they are designed to evangelize the lost and dying. Many will come to a community or home outreach, even if it is Christ centered, because it is a neutral place to have an encounter with God. There are not as many obligations or reservations for a person to attend a Christ-centered outreach when presented for fun and fellowship. Historically women, more than men, love to fellowship with other women. Some of these fellowships include:

- Youth Ministry
- Support Groups
- Dance, Drama and Arts

<u>Youth Ministry</u>

Many female teenagers are tomorrow's torch carriers. Statistics show that most conversions to Christianity occur during adolescence. In reviewing these figures, the importance of youth is very compelling. Young women are a great evangelistic field to be harvested. In childhood, adolescents are subject to parental influence. To a great extent, everyone has a religious belief. During adolescence, teenagers are open to pursuing other dimensions of life. Peer pressure has great influence and when you have a thriving youth ministry it can have a lasting impact. In (*Jeremiah 29:11*) the prophet states,

> *"'For I know the plans I have for you,' says the Lord, 'plans for welfare and not for calamity, to give you a future and a hope.'"*

God has a plan for everyone, especially the younger generation. Many youths today are surrounded by the effects of our declining culture, a society filled with many distractions. A look at the statistics will emphasize the enormous task there is in ministering to today's youth. In the next 24 hours:[1]

- Approximately 1400 teenagers will attempt suicide,
- Approximately 2800 teenage girls will become pregnant,
- Approximately 15,000 teenagers will use drugs for the first time,
- Approximately 3500 babies will be born to unwed mothers,
- Approximately 2900 high school students will drop out of school,

In calculating the daily impact such statistics have on today's youth, it is very plain that there is a need for developing a lasting outreach to them. Prayer is always the first and most essential element needed to begin such an outreach. Most lasting outreaches have a team praying constantly for the leaders and the youths they are to reach. Listed below are some ideas that could be helpful in getting your outreach started.

    a. Explore youth material and information available regarding educational resources. Call different youth organizations, Christian schools/colleges, and develop a database on available books, videos, and Internet resources.

    b. Visit different youth ministry in your community and evaluate what inspired you at those meetings.

    c. Select and conduct your own survey questions regarding the needs for the group of teenagers you want to target. Interview some teenagers and find out what the needs are for your community and surrounding cities.

    d. Take time to develop your vision and goals. *Habakkuk 2:2*
"Write the vision and make it plain on tablets, that he may run who reads it."
The Bible tells us that without a vision, the people perish. It's important to keep the vision and goals for the ministry on the front line, so people can see where God is leading.

The hope is to develop a community in the body of Christ where young people can relate and feel accepted. In a world where they are constantly being confronted regarding their values and their identity, what youth are looking for is unconditional. They, as believers, desperately want unconditional attention, affirmation and encouragement. As believers, we have the answer because God's unconditional love is for all creation. As leaders, this is demonstrated by showing acceptance, a listening ear, God's love and value, and a savior, Christ, who died for her. As role models these issues can be accomplished, and will create a pattern for them to follow. One difficulty is that most youth volunteers are untrained in youth culture. Thus, it is necessary to look for some of the following qualifications in selecting youth workers.

- Select workers that have an interest in teenage girls and have an understanding of the issues they face daily.

- Select workers that have good communication skills, who are good listeners, and are accepting of them unconditionally.
- Select workers who have a commitment to lead teenage girls to know Jesus, how to maintain a lasting relationship with Him, and how to apply Biblical principles to their everyday lives.

After selecting your workers, plan to have training on youth issues, do's and don'ts, and guidelines on acceptable relationships (setting boundaries). Boundaries are very important in relationships, because they set guidelines for everyone, encouraging equal care. It is essential for leaders and volunteers to maintain quality rules for the benefit of the youth group. Counseling should be monitored by trained leaders and should, when applicable, be conducted according to acceptable rules of law. All abuse must be reported to the proper authority. If guidelines are part of your training, there will not be any unresolved issues your group has not addressed in preparing your team.

In selecting a place to have your outreach, remember, environment is essential. Select, if possible, a non-threatening facility that will be inclusive for your youth, to include all Christian and non-Christian youth in the vicinity. Location is everything, because sometimes a church setting can be intimidating. In certain cases, someone's home might be the answer, until your group grows in numbers. One of the most important elements of the location is that you have enough space for interaction before and after meetings. The average teenage girl's attention span is 15 to 20 minutes, so you need to keep the time moving, purposeful, and change topics regularly. Give your teenage girls a reasonable ownership of the meeting, such as having…

- Youth participation in the activities with your guidance,
- Youth hostesses, planning and serving the refreshments,
- Youth praise and worship team, when applicable,
- Youth testimony or teaching approved by leadership,
- Youth leading prayer at the beginning and the end of meeting.

Always take time to evaluate your meetings or events, not only by your volunteers and leaders, but by your youth attendees as well. You will find, if you do this regularly, evaluation will become an important part of your vision, goal, and purpose becoming more fruitful. Of course, the primary issue is whether your youth ministry has presented God's truth, transformational growth, and knowledge of Him fully through the Holy Spirit. The platform you are presenting provides a forum for potential future youth leaders to be trained for the next generation.

Support Groups

Support groups can be an important part of your women's ministry. We know that God's heart is to heal and restore.

(Luke 4:18-19, NJK) "The Spirit of the Lord is upon Me, because He has anointed Me to preach the gospel to the poor, He has sent Me to heal the brokenhearted, to proclaim liberty to the captives and recovery of sight to the blind, to set at liberty those who are oppressed; to proclaim the acceptable year of the Lord."

The New Testament relates to us how Jesus wants to equip the body of Christ to do what He has said in the Scripture. Support groups furnish the time and place where healing the brokenhearted, proclaiming liberty to the captives, and setting at liberty those who are oppressed, can be accomplished. One of the advantages of support groups is the potential for them to be used as evangelistic tools to churched and unchurched women. Women can experience God's healing power at a group setting, it seems, easier than at a church gathering. There are many human problems that can be addressed in a group setting, such as relationships that are broken, issues of self-esteem, guilt and shame, and compulsive behaviors. Since 1980, support groups have grown enormously and continue to be very successful in our society. We can see why support groups continue to be used when we look at some statistics from church adult congregations. [2]

- 22% of women are divorced
- 17% of women are a part of blended families
- 81% have been Christian for 10 years or more
- 75% state that the most important need is spiritual growth
- Only 15% of married couples regularly pray together, other than at meal times.

Support Group Defined

A support group is a group of people meeting for a specific goal, for a limited time, to deal with a common problem. This is not a counseling group. It is be a place for growth and development, where women can learn to apply Biblical principles and take responsibility for making Christ-like choices. The group needs functional accountability, under the supervision of a spiritual leader. Each support group should have guidelines as suggested below:

(Facilitator presents the guidelines)

- Support group attendees are to agree to the three "Cs: Courtesy, Confidentiality, and Christ-centered.

- Support group attendees will begin to communicate through a brief summary of their lives.

- Support group attendees are to give and receive support, not advice. Support group attendees are not to preach or lecture, but can express their feelings and experiences.

Leader Qualifications

The leader of the group should understand conflicts and know how to handle them positively, using essential Biblical patterns.

"Brethren, if any person is overtaken in misconduct or sin of any sort, you who are spiritual (who are responsive to and controlled by the Spirit) should set him right and restore and reinstate him, without any sense of superiority and with all gentleness, keeping an attentive eye on yourself, lest you should be tempted also. Bear (endure, carry) one another's burdens and troublesome moral faults, and in this way fulfill and observe perfectly the law of Christ (the Messiah) and complete what is lacking (in your obedience to it). For if any person thinks himself to be somebody (too important to condescend to shoulder another's load) when he is nobody (of superiority except in his own estimation), he deceives and deludes and cheats himself. But let every person carefully scrutinize and examine and test his own conduct and his own work. He can then have the personal satisfaction and joy of doing something commendable (in itself alone) without (resorting to) boastful comparison with his neighbor."

(Galatians 6:1-4, Amplified)

Remember;

- A Group Facilitator is a role model. She is responsible for motivating and maintaining healthy interaction.
- A Group Facilitator must demonstrate self-disclosure, and is encouraged to self-disclose in the context of a relationship with others.
- A Group Facilitator encourages God's Word and the Holy Spirit's guidance in her interaction with the group.
- A Group Facilitator initiates the exploration of women's struggles to prompt them to discover God's truths.
- A Group Facilitator leads, with wholeness as the goal, acknowledging that change is a process.

Basic communication skills are important in this outreach. The leader needs to have active listening skills to discern what is being said. In order to make sure a facilitator has heard correctly, she should repeat what she thought she was saying to ensure clarification. Try to be personal by using the women's names, which allows a person to feel valued, important and appreciated as they realize that you took the time to memorize their names.

Depending on the qualifications and desires of the available leadership, there are many types of support groups your ministry can decide on for evangelizing. They include (but are not limited to):

- Single Parent Moms
- Military Wives
- Recovery Groups of all kinds. (alcoholics, drug addicts, abuse victims, etc.)
- Dysfunctional Behaviors

Who should be offered the opportunity to join the group? It will depend on the kind of support group your ministry decides to implement. A good rule of thumb is to not have more than ten attendees per group. Your ministry needs to decide if your support group is open for on-going, new attendees, or closed after the group starts. Women that should be excluded from the group are as follows:

- Women who are too busy to attend every session. Attendees should be informed before starting about the importance of attending all meetings, unless there is a dire emergency, because once the group begins, the faithful attendance of each person makes the difference in the effectiveness of the group.
- Women who are not really interested, but are pressured by acquaintances to attend should not participate. Unless they are fully decided this is something they want to participate in they will not likely benefit from the process
- Women who will not be able to keep what they hear confidential. The Bible is clear that gossip can negatively affect a ministry, and women can be hurt by a lack of confidentiality.
- Women who have serious emotional problems. You can best help them by referring them to a licensed therapist and be a prayer partner for them.

Support Groups are a very economical method of helping individuals who may need some counseling, but do not have problems severe enough to warrant individual therapy. The dynamic of group process has been demonstrated to be as effective in most cases as individual therapy. This type of outreach can be effective in building a long-lasting ministry. It demonstrates genuine goodwill and caring, and will attract women who are interested in helping other women in their walk with the Lord.

<u>Dance, Drama and Arts</u>

The Scriptures are full of God's desire for true worship that involves the whole body of Christ in a variety of worship forms where the Holy Spirit has continual freedom, without interference, to bring worshipers into the experience of magnifying God. He can do this most profoundly through dance, drama, and the arts. This can have several dimensions, to include: (from *"Celebrating God through Praise and Worship"*[3])

- Musical instruments – True music is from the heart and not from the head.
  (Colossians 3:16, NKJ) "Let the word of Christ dwell in you richly in all wisdom, teaching and admonishing one another in psalms and hymns and spiritual songs, singing with grace in your hearts to the Lord."

- Song (native language or tongues) – Singing in the Spirit awakens our spirit to the presence of God. singing in a natural melody comes out of a heart full of God's joy.
  (II Corinthians 14;14, NKJ) "…..I will pray with the spirit, and I will also pray with the understanding. I will sing with the spirit, and I will also sing with the understanding."
- Shouting – This is an expression of jubilation and celebration of God.
  (Psalm 132:16, NKJ) "…and the saints shall shout aloud for joy."
- Standing – Worshipping with the whole body.
  (Psalm 135:1-2, NKJ) "…Praise Him, O you servants of the Lord. You who stand in the house of the Lord."
- Lifting Hands –
  (Psalm 134:2, NKJ) "Lift up your hands in the sanctuary and bless the Lord."
- Clapping –
  (Psalm 47:1, NKJ) "O clap your hands, all you people, shout to God with a voice of joy."
- Bowing or Kneeling –
  (Ps 95:6, NKJ) "O come, let us worship and bow down; let us kneel before the Lord our Maker."
- Marching – An acceptable way of Godly worship. *(Joshua 6:2-5)*
- Dancing – Inspired by the Holy Spirit. It can include skipping, whirling, leaping, jumping, includes the whole body, etc.
  (Psalm 149:3, NKJ) "Let them praise His name with a dance."

In the Old Testament, dancing was associated with worship. In modern society, dancing is mostly associated with recreation and worldly activities. As we enter the 21st century, dance, drama and arts are being used in churches for youth activities and outreaches. King David was a worshipper. The Scriptures tell us when he transported the Ark of God that he danced before the Lord *(II Samuel 6:14)*. When Moses and the Israelites were giving God praise after they crossed the Red Sea, Miriam, the Prophetess (the sister of Aaron), took the timbrel in her hand, and all the women went out after her with timbrels and danced before the Lord *(Exodus 15:20)*. These illustrations, movements, and prophetic gestures are expressions of the heart of a worshipper, and they are becoming a more acceptable expression in today's church.

We are living in a day where music has become a tool, especially in our culture, to manipulate mankind. Music is often fueled by the devil to lead people away from the truth of a true worshipper – the truth regarding His redeeming power to set us free and give us everlasting life. The vision of His people should be to equip and train believers to experience the power of Jesus Christ through dance, drama, and arts to impact believers and nonbelievers. Your women's ministry could use this type of ministry to reach your community by having periodic events using prophetic dance teams, drama teams, and processionals of flags and banners. While a person narrates the actions and feelings of a text (scripture interpretation) these performing arts techniques would enhance your evangelistic event immensely. Visual effects provide a lasting impression on the viewers, often reaching the unreachable.

Beginning such a ministry requires prayer and planning. Begin by starting small and enlisting others to help. Form a pilot committee to see if this could be an area your women would be interested in. Let the women know it is a pilot program and your leadership is not certain whether this will be an extensive part of your women's ministry. The arts can be a powerful ministry in which to get children involved. When children want to get involved, they will activate the parents' interest. Usually when this outreach is being considered, the women who are involved in music will be the ones who will step forward to volunteer. Find out in your area where the performing arts are being used. Talk to these women. Let them know you are looking for someone to help with choreography. Present the needs of the outreach to your group when your committee meets for the first time. Listed below are a few suggestions for your planning.

- Begin to prepare the vision, purpose and plan to implement this task.
- Select a leader to coordinate the performing arts activities. (Sometimes you will find the coordinator will need an assistant who has administrative abilities to take care of incidentals. Quite often there is a need for assistance to leadership.)
- Set prayer times - Times set aside for waiting on the Lord with dedicated volunteers.

- Begin to select skits and stories – Have each of the committee members spend time preparing a presentation to present to the committee with scripture and props, so the committee can input their comments before the event.
- Prepare a budget – Have the committee members make an evaluation of the cost.

As you progress in the development of an arts ministry, much information can be found on the internet, such as the significance of colors and symbols, Tribes of Israel (symbols, ministry gifting and colors), the significance of the flags being presented in your pageantry, etc. (From *http://wcpageantry.com*) For example, the charts on pages 175 and 176 provide a glimpse at some symbolic aspects of God and His word that could be a part of dance, drama, and arts.

Flags – Symbol of High Calling to Usher in the Presence of God

Interpretation of the flag bearer – Many worshippers using flags are inspired by God and interpret their moving of the flags accordingly to the moving of the Holy Spirit. In their presentation, the interpretation of the colors of the flag (colors listed above) are determined by prophetic discernment of God's flowing in the service. Sometimes it is warfare and wrestling against powers in the heavens.

Prophetic Gestures

Interpretation of prophetic gestures may be found in *"Study in Biblical Communication."*[4]

Lively Arts

Interpretation of the lively arts may be found in *"Praising God Through the Lively Arts"*[5] This book provides Scripture interpretation, drama, storytelling, liturgical dance, choral Scripture readings, dancing positions, sacred hand movement, costumes, skits. Hopefully the information referenced above will be contributing factors to helping your women's ministry pursue the "lively arts" as an outreach in your community.

In Jeremiah, the Scriptures talk about the New Covenant promised by God. The Lord reveals His future plan where there will be praise and worship, to include dancing to celebrate the presence of the Lord with His people.

"...Again you shall take up your tambourines, and go forth to the dances of the merrymakers." (verse 13) "...the maidens shall rejoice in the dance..." (Jeremiah 31:4 & verse 13, NAS)

COLORS

Color	Interpretation	Scripture
Amber/Gold	Glory of God	Ezekiel 1:4, Ezekiel 8:2
Black	Sin, affliction, calamity	Lam. 4:8
	Death, famine, mourning	Jeremiah. 8:21
	Evil, omen, humiliation	Zechariah. 6:2, Malachi 3:14
		Revelation 6:5
Bronze/Brass	Judgment	Micah 4:13, Revelation 2:18
Red (flame)	Blood, life, atonement	Isaiah 1:18
(scarlet)	Sin, sacrifice	Joshua 2:18-19
(crimson)	Consuming fire	Leviticus 14:52
Blue	Heaven, heavenly	Exodus 24:10
(hyacinth)	Holy Spirit, Reward	Numbers 15:38
	Divine Relation	Ezekiel 1:26
Green	Freshness, vigor	Psalm 92:14
	Life, prosperity	Psalm 37:35
Purple	Kingship, Majesty	John 19:2
	Royalty	Judges 8:26
Silver	Redemption	Matthew 27:28
White	Festivity, triumph, light	Ecclesiastes 9:8
	Purity, righteousness	Daniel 7:9
	Salvation, holiness, glory	Zechariah 6:3, Matthew 17:2,
		John 20:12, Revelation 6:2,
		Revelation 7:9, Revelation 19:8

The Tribes of Israel (symbols, ministry gifting and colors)

Tribe	Meaning	Ministry
Judah –	Praise *(Genesis 49:8)*	Worship Ministry (Lion)
	Color: Emerald/Green	
Issachar –	Man of Hire *(Genesis 49:14-15)*	Serving Motive (Donkey)
	Color: Amethyst/Purple	
Zebulin –	Dwelling *(Genesis 49:13)*	The Apostles (Ships)
	Color: Aquamarine/Blue-Green	
Reuben –	Behold a Son *(Genesis 49:3)*	The Leadership Motive
	Color: Ruby/Red	
Simeon –	Hearing *(Genesis 29:33)*	The Mercy Motive (Sword)
	Color: Topaz/Yellow	
Gad –	Good Fortune *(Genesis 49:19)*	Evangelists (Spiritual-Prayer Warrior)
	Color: Jacinth/Orange	
Levi –	Joined *(Deuteronomy 10:8)*	Exhortation Motive (Priestly Tribe called to teach and exhort)
	Color: Garnet/Dark Red	
Joseph –	Increaser *(Genesis 49:22-24)*	The Pastors (Shock of Wheat)
	Color: Onyx/Black	
Benjamin –	Son of My Right Hand *(Gen 49:27)*	Administration Motive (Wolf)
	Color: Jasper/Blackish Green	
Dan –	Judge *(Genesis 49:16)*	The Prophets (Balance Scales)
	Color: Sapphire/Blue	

The Scriptures are clear that dancing is an important part of worship, to be used for the Glory of God. Those who lead praise have an awesome responsibility to the Lord to use their talents to fight the forces of darkness. The Lord will equip them and give them His strength to bring joy and victory. Dance, drama, and arts can be a mighty evangelistic tool to be used to set people free and bring them into the kingdom of God for His glory. It is well worth the time and effort to seek out the Lord's plan for an outreach into your area of influence as a cutting edge ministry to children, youth, and young and old alike.

References

[1] Every Day in America. *The Children Defense Fund.* http//www.childrendefense.org/everyday.htm, April 2001

[2] Jim Burns/Mike Devries (2003). *Parenting with Parents.* Gospel Light Publishing.

[3] John McGeorge,. *Celebrating God through Praise & Worship.* Ministry to Eastern Europe, Inc., Richmond, VA

[4] Todd Farley (1989). *Study in Biblical Communication.* Destiny Image Publishers

[5] Linda M. Goens (1999). *Praising God through the Lively Arts.* Library of Congress.

End of Chapter Questions

Chapter 10

1. Name some qualifications for selecting youth workers.
2. What are some of the ways you can give teenage girls part ownership in youth ministry?
3. What guidelines should a "support group" have to facilitate a meeting?
4. Name some qualifications for leadership of a "support group."
5. What are some ways to celebrate God in worship? Give an interpretation of each one.
6. How do you personally see the importance of dance, drama, and arts in modern day evangelism?

Chapter 11: *Conferences & Retreats*

If you took a survey of most women's ministries, large or small, you would find they have conferences and retreats usually once or twice a year. The reason for having conferences and retreats is that they offer many opportunities for evangelizing, versatile teaching, and spiritual growth. Conferences can vary in length from one day to a week, and can meet in a church, hotel room, or a community facility. If women will be coming from a long distance, then local hotel arrangements will have to be made available.

A retreat is usually an overnight event held in a retreat center or resort. They are quite similar in that they have main speakers, preaching, teaching and workshops, but usually retreats allow more time for recreation and fellowship. As we explore both, for the sake of referring to the words conferences or retreats, the information regarding this subject matter will be addressed as meetings. These meetings/gatherings not only can be a spiritual growth for the body of Christ, but also an evangelistic encounter.

"If My people who are called by My name will humble themselves, and pray, and seek My face, and turn from their wicked ways, then I will hear from heaven, and will forgive their sins and heal their lands." *(II Chronicles 7:14, NKJ)*

Let's explore how these meetings can be used to start a revival. In the beginning stages of your planning, your ministry group should start with the steps of prayer for revival. Who knows if an outpouring like you have never anticipated might occur! Theses steps are adapted from the booklet, *"Steps to Revival,"* by Pat Robertson.[1]

A. <u>Steps to Revival</u> There are six steps to revival. They are:
1. Humility – In revival you will find that the Lord will first refine and purify His people and fill them with His power. *(James 4:6b, NKJ)*

    "...God opposes the proud, but gives grace to the humble."

    Revival usually starts with Christians and then affects the surrounding areas.

2. Prayer – In revival, without prayer your meetings aren't going anywhere. When prayer is consistent, lives will be transformed. *(II Chronicles 7:15, NKJ)*

"Now My eyes will be open and My ears attentive to prayer, made in this place."

Travailing is what touches the heart of God.

3. Seeking God's Face – In revival, seeking God's face and His plan is like entering into a new relationship with Him.

    "But we all, with unveiled face, beholding as in a mirror the glory of the Lord, are being transformed into the same image from glory to glory, just as by the Spirit of the Lord." (II Corinthians 3:18, NKJ)

4. Turn From Our Wicked Ways – Before revival there needs to be a turning from our wicked ways to be cleansed from all unrighteousness. If our hearts are hardened we need to repent and turn back to the Lord. *(Psalm 139:23a, NKJ)*

    "Search me, O God, and know my heart..."

5. Unity – In revival unity is vital to the success of your endeavors. Many women's ministries have started in a small room in a home with several women dedicated to spending time to seek out God's vision for their course of action. The same is true regarding any meetings. Without the unity of believers gathering together for the purpose of seeking God's plan little will happen. Without an anticipation of a visitation of His divine revelation can the purpose of reaching the lost and dying be accomplished? *(Ephesians 4:1-3, NKJ)*

    "I .....beseech you to walk worthy of the calling with which you were called, with all lowliness and gentleness, with long suffering, bearing with one another in love, endeavoring to keep the unit of the Spirit in the bond of peace."

6. Perseverance - In revival, these steps can all be taken, but without perseverance to continue with some effort toward a course of action, steadfast in purpose, the event will abort before the vision and goal of your meetings will take place. There is a great need to press in and wait for God and He will give you the revelation knowledge and strength to complete the task He has set before you. *(Matthew 9:37-38, Amplified)*

    "...The Harvest is indeed plentiful, but the laborers are few. So pray to the Lord of the harvest to force out and thrust laborers into His harvest."

The Scriptures make it clear how important is to start with a group of women who have humbled themselves, praying and seeking God, purifying and cleansing themselves to hear from the Lord the purpose and plan for the event. After prayerfully selecting your committee of women for planning, the next step is planning and using a timeline to accomplish the necessary tasks.

B. <u>Planning</u>
   1. Confirm Your Date and Location – When confirming the date and location for the meeting, you should have at least a year before the event. It is most important that you consult your church calendar and when you select the date put it on the church calendar so if other functions are being planned they will not select your designated date. If the meeting is being held elsewhere, be sure you select a date compatible with other ministries in your group or church events. Another thing to remember is to be sure you don't select a date that will conflict with a holiday. This will also ensure more availability for your selected audience.

      If the location is at the church, the task will be easier, but if it is to be held at another location, planning for the date will take more coordination. Occasionally your audience for the event will be a deciding factor for facilitating the affair at other places. Many women will find it more convenient to attend a conference or retreat if it is located in the surrounding areas, because if attendees are from other churches it can be a neutral location for them.
   2. Theme – The theme is important and should be decided as soon as possible after the date and location is determined. As you prayerfully consider the theme, a Scripture reference is important. Your theme should weave as a thread the message God has given you and your ministry's vision. You will find that the seminar or itinerant speakers you might select will want to know what God is saying to your group and then they will decide what to speak on accordingly.
   3. Speakers – Ask God to reveal to your women who has the message and is in harmony with the direction for your ministry at this time. After forming your list, begin to pray specifically for the Lord's confirmation on His choice. Have your pastor or ministry advisors give you their input after praying and getting the heart of

God. When you write a letter to the speaker make sure you include all information she will need to make her decision. It is important for the prospective speaker to know the following information:

- The speaker's honorarium (love gift) should be determined by the number of times she will be speaking during the allotted times during your meetings. This should be decided before sending the letter. Ask her if this amount is satisfactory or does she require certain speaking fees. This will depend on the reputation of the speaker. The more well-known her reputation is, the larger the honorarium you should expect to give.
- The speaker's transportation arrangements and expenses are usually made by the speaker in advance and they will submit a report to your ministry. Make sure this is planned for in your budget.
- Speakers sometimes request accommodations for a traveling companion. This is not unusual, so be prepared to have your committee decision on this matter be decided in advance. Most speakers that request a traveling companion will include their accommodations.

4. Workshops – Usually the main speaker will do one or two workshops. In selecting the other workshop speakers, try to select someone in your women's ministry. This helps to develop your ministry internally and give your leaders an opportunity to use their giftings. Select mature Christian women who are dedicated to serving and are continually inspired by the Holy Spirit. Whenever possible, try to include as many women as possible in your ministry to be a part of the volunteer selections. You will find they will promote the success of your meeting. Workshop speakers should receive a love gift, even if it is small. Sometimes scholarships (partial or full) are advisable as a part of their love gift. After selecting each workshop speaker, make sure they submit an outline of their designated subject matter. This is important to ensure a flow of the workshops, to make sure the teaching is compatible with the theme and harmony in your meeting.

5. Worship Leader – Worship is one of the most powerful and purest forms of communication with God. That is why it is so important to select dedicated worshippers to encourage the power of His Spirit in the meeting. Good worship

will help set the atmosphere for the Holy Spirit to reveal His revelation knowledge, heart-to-heart. If possible, in your women's ministry, you should try to have a women's worship team already established. If not, interview worship teams who have a heart for the Lord and will willingly accept an opportunity to bring worship to your meeting.

6. Budget – Once the costs of the location and speakers are determined, a budget for the retreat should be made. Each committee leader will need to submit her costs for her particular area of responsibility, so the overall budget can be established. This should include lodging (if needed), meals (if furnished), material handouts, speakers' honorariums, and other miscellaneous costs incurred. Each event is different, so you cannot determine the total needed until all costs are designated. Some costs may need to be estimated in order to proceed with printing brochures and to send out registration request forms.

7. Brochures – In putting your brochure together, after all the information is decided, your committee will have decisions to make as to the type of brochure, color, print, enhancing the theme, presented in an attractive way. People are visual, and how you present your meeting will enhance your marketing effort. Advertisement and publicity are another big part of marketing your event. In Appendix 3 there is an example of a brochure you can use. It is good planning to have your brochures ready four months ahead of the event and in the hands of your volunteers for promotion.

8. Committee/Coordination Chairwoman – She has the responsibility of keeping a time line and budget constants established, so she can maintain how each project is developing, and oversee the other designated chairwomen, such as:

    - Reservation Chairwoman – Responsible for taking reservations, collecting the monies, enforcing rules for cancellation deadlines. Select and train volunteers to be available at the entrance of the meeting to check in each attendee as she arrives. At that time, make appropriate name tags and hand out packet/folders to each woman.
    - Audio/visual Chairwoman – Responsible for taking care of the equipment needed for worship and speakers and recording all sessions of meetings.

- Publicity Chairwoman – Responsible for advertising the meeting through newspaper ads, radio or TV announcements, if available. Selecting and training women for making calls to invite and encourage prospective attendees.

- Decoration Chairwoman – Responsible for arriving at the meeting early to set up decorations and staying after meeting is completed to dismantle. Selecting and decorating the room are an important part of setting the mood for the theme, making it inviting to the attendees.

- Packet Chairwoman – Responsible for putting the attendee's packet/folders together with all the information for speakers outlines, local eating places (if applicable), vicinity maps, agenda for the meeting (including workshop times), evaluation card, or any other information the attendee might need regarding the meeting.

- Prayer Chairwoman – Responsible for overseeing women who will be praying every day for the meeting and a time schedule for prayer times. Prayers include praying for the speakers, chairwomen, attendees, and any other prayer-specific requests that have been submitted to the prayer chairwoman.

- Counseling Chairwoman – Responsible to have a trained team to minister with leaders (if desired), and responsible for handing out decision (salvation acceptance) cards, follow-up information cards, and any other prayer counseling needs.

- Books/Tapes/CD/VDD Chairwoman – Responsible to set up and maintain all sales of ministry materials or well-known Christian authors and speakers material that is being sold.

- Greeters/Ushers Chairwoman – Responsible to train greeters to make welcome and give directions to attendees when needed. Train ushers to usher the attendees (if needed) to be seated and be ready to collect offerings.

- Offering Chairwoman – Responsible to prepare an offering message usually presented after praise and worship. The message should be prayerfully prepared and be presented in a timely manner. After the ushers collect the offering, the main usher presents the offering to the chairwoman. She is responsible for counting the offering (with at least one other person) and preparing the offering tally as instructed by the committee coordinator.

Other activities that may be needed, but may not require a Chairwoman, include:
- Conference/Retreat – Examples of a Timeline and Budget are provided in Appendices 4 and 5. Periodically, through the planning of your event, it is necessary to have staff meetings. The Committee/Coordinator Chairwoman has the responsibility to conduct meetings with all the designated Chairwomen to ensure unity by keeping all involved informed of the overall tasks being implemented for this event. When volunteers for the project are kept informed, they will continue to pledge their loyalty to the success of the event.
- Communion – It is an option whether you want to have communion as part of one of your meetings. Some women's ministries may want a clergyman present to conduct the communion service. Usually communion will take place during the first night of the meeting or the last meeting. It is up to your discretion whether you want a clergyman present to conduct the service or whether one of your leaders will present the communion. Some ministries have advisors (who are generally pastors) who are used for consulting and are on their Advisory Board. Having an advisor (pastor) to perform the sacraments is one option and keeps your advisors committed to the ministry.

C. Follow Up

In any ministry, follow-up after an event is a great evangelistic tool. In your packet/folder that will be presented to the attendees upon arrival, there should be an evaluation sheet. It should be announced during the meeting that you would like your attendees to fill out the evaluation as an aid to plan for future events. These evaluations are very helpful. Another helpful information tool is the decision cards and prayer cards your attendees fill out, so that your leadership can follow up on these women. Several ways to follow up are:

1. A personal hand-written card sent to encourage the new believers.

2. A personal phone call to encourage them, and ask them if you may pray for them or serve them in other ways.
3. A personal invitation to your next women's meeting. Send the announcement in the mail with a hand-written note.
4. A friendly visit, after you have made a personal contact over a casual lunch or dinner.
5. A personal acknowledgment if they do decide to attend your next meeting. Name tags at each meeting are important so that you would be aware if your follow up contact was helpful. Try to remember names; it makes women feel they are important, because you remembered them in a personal way

After follow-up contact has been made, continue to mentor the women and disciple them. The commission of Christ is to make disciples, not just converts. So the objective after you have made your relationship secure, is to help the women in their progress to become Christ-like. This will give her that assurance her spiritual life is secure in Him.

(II Corinthians 5:17, Amplified) "Therefore if any person is (ingrafted) in Christ (the Messiah) he is a new creation (a new creature altogether); the old (previous moral and spiritual condition) has passed away. Behold, the fresh and new has come."

D. <u>Post-Planning</u>

After your event, a time known as "*Afterglow*" is appropriate. This is time well spent, reliving the highlights of the event and experiencing the love, joy and appreciation of the speakers, volunteers, and attendees' participation in the event. But most of all, it is a time to give thanks that God orchestrated and directed every area in His divine way. It's such a blessing when your ministry accomplishes an event with a great anointed evangelistic outreach. This is also a time to reflect on how to better serve your ministry in the future.

Then (after a short interval) it is important for your ministry to have a meeting of all leaders and chairwomen to formulate a plan for the next year's event, while it is still fresh in their minds. Final reports of each planning stage for each function needs to be submitted to leadership, so that they have an evaluation of what transpires during the planning stage. Some chairwomen and volunteers will probably return for the next event, but there are seasons in their lives for participation, and perhaps next year some will not be available. To prevent guesswork in the planning for your next event, have each leader and chairwomen submit a final report. This is valuable information in establishing budgets for each task and getting suggestions on what worked and didn't work during the time line. Why reinvent the wheel, when others have experience and knowledge in certain areas? A report compiled by a designated coordinator of all these facts will save duplicating hours of planning your next event.

In conclusion, these suggestions and planning ideas have been successfully administered in the past and will continue to be valuable in the future to your ministry. Each conference and retreat is different, but they all have the same message to reach the lost in a world that is crying out for help. Giving women of your ministry an opportunity to be used in the kingdom of God is an awesome legacy and inheritance of what Jesus did for us.

(I Corinthians 15:58, NKJ) "Therefore, my beloved brethren, be steadfast, immovable, always abounding in the work of the Lord, knowing that your labor is not in vain in the Lord."

Reference:
[1] Pat Robertson Ministry (2001). *Steps to Revival*. Pamphlet.

End of Chapter Questions
Chapter 11

1. Name the six steps to revival and give a brief description of each one.
2. Why is it so important to have a timeline for an event?
3. Name the committees suggested to perform the task of planning.
4. What committee would you elect to be on and why?
5. Why is follow-up on a conference or retreat so valuable? Name some follow-up suggestions.
6. Why is post-planning after an event so important?

Chapter 12 *Prison Ministry & Re-Entry Programs*

There is a large and growing missionary field today that has exploded in our society throughout our nation. It involves ministering the Gospel message in prisons, jails, re-entry facilities, and with children who have parents involved in the criminal system. Never in the history of society has there been such an evangelistic field made available to "who-so-ever-will"! The call and mandate is staggering after looking at the statistics listed below from *"Correction Today:"* [1]

- An estimated 1.4 million inmates are housed in American's state and federal prisons. (This doesn't include county jails)
- These inmates are parents of 1.5 million children. The majority of these children range between the ages of 1 and 10.
- The number of inmates that will re-enter society this year (2004) is approaching 700,000.

There are different ways to involve yourselves with this growing population. Your women's ministry can get involved in, such as Bible Studies, Christian Growth and Development Classes, One-on-One mentoring, visiting inmates incarcerated in prisons/jails, Re-Entry Facilities, Mentoring Programs, and children's programs provided by non-profit groups. These are all available opportunities for ministering. There are many ways you can be a role model, showing love and compassion for women struggling with life's problems. Jesus talked about judgment when He comes in His glory and the importance of helping people in need.

(Matthew 40:25, NKJ)"…inasmuch as you did it to one of the least of these, My brethren, you did it to Me."

There is such a great need to help women offenders during their restoration into society. What a blessing it is to see women restored and united with their families.

A. How to Develop and Maintain a Prison Ministry [2]
  1. As a leader who is exploring avenues of ministry for your group, start by getting a group of women together (who you think would like to be involved in this outreach) and pray. If your women are interested, the call from the Lord will be strong and the mandate will be compelling.

2. Contact country/state jails or prisons in your area and set up an appointment to meet with the chaplain in charge of that facility to see what his needs are. Consolidate the needs and present it to your women who are praying about this outreach.

3. Meet with your group and have a presentation of the chaplain's needs for the inmates and provide an opportunity for your women's input. If the vision, goals and purpose of this outreach take form, seek God's endorsement as you continue to plan.

4. Find other ministries in your area that are involved in prison ministry. Visit the group to see how they facilitate their meetings and training. There is no need to duplicate a ministry that has already developed a n effective program.

5. Start small! Develop your own training, and train a small group, then call the chaplain and inform him you are ready to start a Bible study. Each facility has their own training that is required before entering their facility. Have your group complete the application with the facility so the necessary security check on each woman can be accomplished. Also develop your own application with information pertinent for your screening. As an example, modify the same application your ministry required for leadership described in Chapter 5. Be sure you have the husband's permission (if the woman is married) or her pastor's acknowledgment of her involvement. When going into a facility, the women should have at least two people praying for her.

6. Rules to Follow – Not only does the facility you are ministering in have rules or boundaries, but your group should also set rules for themselves and future trainees (as you build your team), such as;

    - No phone calls are to be made to outside contacts from inmates, nor are messages to be delivered or brought in. Inform the inmate it is against the facilities rules and any violation could result in termination of the ministry from the facility.

    - No personal information is to be disclosed to the inmate; use your first names only. If an inmate wants to contact you after release, give them your church phone number or address. Then inform your church not to give out your information, but ask for a number where the ex-inmate can be reached for contact.

- Do not make inquiries regarding an inmate's personal status. If the inmate wants to inform you how she got into the correctional system that is done at her discretion. We are not there to judge, only to minister Christ's redemptive love.
- Take no restroom visits alone, unless a deputy escorts you or you have permission before the meeting to have one of your group escort you.
- No team member should be in the meeting room alone. The Lord sent them out two by two and that is an example your team should follow. Even the deputies require more than one team member in the room at all times.
- Always remember you are a guest and should obey their instructions. Through keeping this commitment you will find your team will be respected. Remember, the inmates are always looking to you, as a model, being an ambassador for Christ.
- You are there to present Christ and should only present His gospel, not your doctrine. Let the Lord orchestrate and administer His message pertinent to her life's issues. Handouts are important, but must be cleared by the chaplain. Keep your Bible handy at all times so that you can refer to a Bible reference if needed.
- Appearance is important and so is hygiene. Use discretion when it comes to appropriate dress. If you dress modestly, it will not take the attention off your presentation or Christ.

These are some suggested rules to get you started. Many adjustments can be made along the way to facilitate your goals in the ministry.

7. Monthly or bi-monthly meetings should be conducted with your group. This is a time for team members to share what works and what doesn't. There should be a short training regarding issues of the prison ministry. At these meetings you could invite women who are interested in joining your group. There should be meeting attendance requirement for new members, before presenting a time for training them. If the women are committed they will attend regularly until the leadership of your

group decides she is ready to join your team. Prayer is vital in the prison meetings and each team member should be prayed for and ministered to. This encourages the team members and demonstrates the value of their endeavors. Further, it helps them to stay focused on the importance of ministering at all levels to women that are incarcerated.

8. Prayer Group – As you expand into other facilities, the ministry should have a prayer group that prays for each facility. Prayer covering before, during, and after the meeting in the facility is essential. The enemy of our souls would love to attack before, during, and after a meeting, especially when lives are being changed. Some women will not want to minister in the jails/prison, but are called to pray. These women are "watchmen on the wall," protecting the ministry through prayer. Also, these women need prayer too, and should be ministered to periodically from leadership. They can come under attack as well and should have at least two people praying for them. A healthy ministry is a praying ministry.

9. Pen Pal – Let your pen be your pulpit! Another important part of Prison Ministry is writing letters to inmates. Your team members, who are ministering in the facility, will not be able to write to an inmate. Those are the rules of the facility. But you can solicit other women in your ministry to write an encouraging letter. This is an awesome way to minister Christ while staying at home. Many older women, who really do not desire to travel, find this part of the ministry very rewarding. A letter is something to put into the inmates' hand that they can read and re-read over and over again when they get discouraged. It also provides opportunity for inmates to write and ask questions they want answers to regarding the Bible. Be sure to caution your women not to preach to the inmates, but rather befriend them. The chaplain of the facility will provide the ground rules for your pen pal women to follow, but the more important part of writing is being able to express God's working power in your life and the lives of others. A Post Office Box will be needed for this part of the ministry, because you do not want to give the inmates your home address, just as a precaution, for the safety of everyone involved. A designated woman could be responsible for picking up the letters from the Post Office Box and distributing them

to the pen pal writers. You and your ministry will be blessed by participating in doing this project as part of your prison ministry outreach.

10. Training – New team members will definitely need training. It is a good policy to have the other members attend and possibly share their experiences. Training should be offered periodically, depending on the discretion of leadership. You will find that having these ongoing trainings always strengthens the cohesiveness of your group. When they hear the testimonies of the inmates being shared by the team members, they become inspired and revitalized.

11. Materials – In selecting your materials for prison ministry you need to assess your audience. You will find in the jails that many of the inmates do not have much education. By the time some of these inmates are sent to prison, they have acquired their GED (equivalent to a high-school diploma) and are reading at a higher level. Some are well educated, so your team will have to evaluate each situation. In the beginning it is better to start with basic Biblical foundation material, such as a salvation message, Christ's character, Christ's parables, Biblical characters. Some will know the Bible and others may have never been exposed to its content. Take into consideration that jail time is from one month to one year. So the chances are that these inmates may be with you for one meeting or several, depending on the duration of their incarceration. Do not miss an opportunity to present a salvation message to them.

In some prisons the inmates are there for 15 years to life. If you know the inmates are going to be there for a while, your team may do a series of teachings, such as A Book of the Bible (chapter by chapter), a series on Biblical principles, a series on the authority of the believer, Christian life, Covenants of God, kingdom living, etc. Teachings can be on anything that provides an in-depth study of Christian traditions. These studies give the new converts a solid base in Christian principles. Many inmates have poor self-esteem, so teaching on "Who They Are in Christ" can be a life-changing experience. Keep it simple and interesting by dividing your allotted time into three components (Praise & Worship, teaching the lesson, and praying for the needs of the inmates). It has been proven over and over again that these three components have the best results in a prison/jail setting.

12. Qualifications for a prison team member should never be taken lightly. Here are some of the qualifications the group should be looking for in a team member.

   a. The team member should have a deep relationship with the Lord, professing Christ as their Savior with fruit of maturity in their work.

   b. The team member should have a good ability to interpret Scriptures clearly. Key Scriptures pertinent to fundamental truths should be available for easy access when questions are being asked.

   c. The team member should know the importance of prayer, especially knowing how to pray the Scriptures over their prayee. Knowing the power of prayer and their authority in Christ is essential.

   d. The team member should take time to get acquainted with the inmate. Know her personality and her ability to communicate her Christian walk with the Lord.

   e. The team member should always remember that confidential information is not to be repeated. Trust is a big issue with inmates.

   f. The team member should maintain her good behavior when an inmate is displaying anger, malice, or discontentment. Mirror back to the inmate the right attitude to diffuse uncontrolled behavior.

   g. The team member should have the attitude of a servant, being sensitive rather than judgmental. Be accepting at all times and listen with the ear of the Lord to give sound Biblical advice and counsel.

13. Deliverance – In prison ministry work you may face the need for deliverance. According to your women's ministry belief statement on the subject, you should have guidelines to ensure your team members are trained in this area. Every facility's chaplain will have his own belief on deliverance and will be the deciding factor whether it can be ministered. Remember, your ministry reports to the chaplain of the facility and you are responsible to follow their rules. Many chaplains know the value of inmates being delivered from demonic spirits. It is necessary that you take authority over the spirits in the name of Jesus. However, some chaplains have

their preferred ways of administering deliverance and healing to the inmate. We need to be mature and balanced in our understanding of spiritual, emotional, and physical causes of problems. Not everything is a demon. Your team members need to ask the Lord for discernment and wisdom.

When administering deliverance, address the issue as a "Strongman." The Bible clearly teaches on this concept.

> *(Matthew 12:29, NKJ) "Or else how can one enter into a strong man's house and spoil his goods, unless first he binds the strong one, and then he will plunder his house."*
>
> *(Matthew 18:18, NJK) "Assuredly, I say to you, whatsoever you bind on earth will be bound in heaven, and whatever you loose on earth will be loosed in heaven."*
>
> *(John 10:10, NKJ) Jesus said: "The thief does not come except to steal and to kill, and to destroy, I have come that they may have life, and that they may have it more abundantly."*

By recognizing the spirits as strongmen in their lives and knowing which strongman is to be bound and cast out, the enemy of our soul can be defeated. Be careful when praying for the inmates that you don't frighten them. Some new believers may be anxious about the idea of a "strongman" in their life. It may help to define them as attitudes within us. Do not try to administer deliverance to a non-believer. God is a God of love and He will administer deliverance and healing in miraculous ways. We just need to be obedient to His call and be ready for all situations that may arise in these facilities.

Shown in the table on the following page are some strongmen that you might encounter during ministry:[3]

If more assistance in forming your prison ministry is needed, write the author and she will endeavor to help you or point you in the right direction.

Strongmen in Spiritual Warfare

Name	Description	Deliverance Scripture
• Bondage Spirit	(Addictions, drugs, alcohol, etc.)	Romans 8:15
• Securing Spirit	(Deception, entices, false prophets)	John 16:13
• Spirit of Fear	(Anxiety, stress, torment, nightmares)	2 Timothy 1:7
• Deaf & Dumb Spirit	(Seizures, suicidal, crying, dumb)	Romans 8:11
		2 Corin. 12:9
• Spirit of Jealousy	(Anger, hate, murder, revenge)	1 Corin. 13
		Eph. 5:2
• Spirit of Haughtiness	(Pride, arrogance, rebellion)	Proverbs. 16:19
		Romans 1:4
• Spirit of Divination	(Fortuneteller, hypnotist, magic)	1 Corin. 12:9-12
• Familiar Spirit	(Spiritist, clairvoyant, medium)	1 Corin. 12:9-12
• Spirit of Error	(False doctrines, unteachable)	1 John 4:6
		Ps. 51:10
• Lying Spirit	(Strong deception, lies, gossip)	John 14:17; 15:26; 16:13
• Spirit of Heaviness	(Self-pity, depression, insomnia)	John 15:26
		Isaiah 61:3
• Spirit of Infirmity	(Lingering disorders, allergies)	Romans 8:2
		1 Corin. 12:9
• Spirit of Whoredoms	(Unfaithfulness, idolatry, adultery)	Ephesians 3:16
• Spirit of Anti-Christ	(Against Christ, deceiver)	1 John 4:6

B. Re-entry Programs

Another vital part of inmates becoming ex-inmates is their re-entry into society. This is where the rubber meets the road! The statistics show that over 80% of the jail/prison population will return to prison if there isn't a support group available. The first 24 hours are most critical for the ex-inmate after their release from jail/prison. With women, it is even harder because most women have children and the caregivers (if court ordered) cannot release the children back to the ex-inmate unless they have a home and the ability to provide for children. This can be overwhelming for a woman in this situation. Their driver's license was taken away upon arrest, so they need to reapply. Usually, if they are put on parole/probation, there is a mandate to report to their appointed officer within 24 hours. If the ex-inmate doesn't have anywhere to go, they will need to find shelter. Without an address how can they get a job? The magnitude of such enormous decisions goes on and on, with everything becoming too much to handle for the ex-convict. That is why re-entry programs are so important in the lives of women being placed back into society Thus, it is important to pool resources together. Your women's ministry could be one of the resources, but let us look at the most important needs first. There are three important dynamics to recovery: Spirituality, Education, and Community (Re-Entry)[4]

1. Spirituality – It is important for true rehabilitation that the realization of becoming a new creation in Christ is the most important step. Complete restoration can only take place after salvation and true repentance.

    (II Corinthians 5:17-18, NKJ) "Therefore if any man be in Christ, he is a new creature; old things are passed away; behold all things are become new. And all things are of God, who has reconciled us to himself by Jesus Christ, and has given us the ministry of reconciliation."

The individual must realize they are powerless and only through the empowerment of Christ can they live an overcoming life in today's world. With so many distractions pulling them back into old habits a strong spiritual foundation is essential. Starting with spirituality is the first step. Your ministry can be an integral part of this by continuing to mentor the ex-offender, helping them to see change through Christ, change from her former associations and change to a new environment. There are many good examples of Christians modeling Christ.

Everyone should strive to be one of them. Example is the best testimony in today's world.

2. Education – The lack of social skills can be major problem in learning how to cope, solve problems, and learn the fundamentals of maturity. The only way to solve these human development skills is by assisting the ex-offender to gain knowledge. General developmental stages people normally experience in childhood and teen years will need to be addressed. A plan to assist in overcoming arrested development is needed. Issues to overcome or enhance include:

   - Communication skill with every part of society, home, surrounding environment and work. Many ex-offenders do not have the ability to maintain the stability and confidence needed to communicate effectively.
   - Crisis (any kind of crisis), in different situations in their lives as they are being rehabilitated. Learning to develop coping skills when fear, rejection and loneliness (just to address a few) occur in daily life is needed.
   - Developing a perception of one's self worth. Learning to develop self worth through who Christ said they are, not society. Self-worth is needed to find their potential in Christ.

   These are just some of the re-educational needs the ex-offender will face. Establishing an After Care Group in your prison ministry outreach would greatly enhance the chances of ex-offenders' recovery into society. Monthly meetings addressing these issues and training them how to maintain in difficult times would be very helpful.

3. Community – A healing community for the ex-offender could be the greatest "arm of society," stretching out a hand to help someone in need. Everyone needs family. Whether it is natural born family, support group family, or a church family, most chaplains will agree, if every church would adopt just one ex-offender into their church community there would be a 50% reduction of them returning to jail/prison. Former inmates need to be with mature people who will spend time with them and help support them in areas that are pertinent to their assimilation into society. Ex-offenders have many needs and it will take a committed group of people to love on them and treat them with respect.

It takes all three dynamics to recovery (Spirituality, Education, and Community). If one is missing, it is like a three-legged stool that has a leg missing. It will become unstable and will not function properly. After-Care Groups are vital. If your ministry could become one of these groups, it would be life-changing to both the ex-inmates and to those in your ministry.

Another area of help that your women's prison ministry could provide is a resource book. The book provides many available resources to ex-inmates that can be found in your surrounding communities. This would be a great service for ex-offenders. Although your ministry may not have many of the resources needed, you can supply information on resources available, such as:

- Churches – Before listing churches, call them and tell them you would like to put their church name/address as a resource for people in need.
- Rehabilitation & Recovery Organizations – A list of their name/address and type of facility and services they offer.
- Temporary Housing/Shelter – Information on how long they can stay at different facilities.
- Maternity Housing and Issues – Some places cater to pregnant women and train them on life's issues.
- Employment – There are agencies that help women to construct a resume, give them employment contacts, and help train them to get a job in the community.
- Social Services – Public assistance information, such as; Welfare, AFDC, medical, food stamps, etc.
- Financial Assistance – There are some community services that give financial aid for a limited time.

Another area of service needs based upon staggering statistics is the need to help the children of incarcerated women. According to the BJS report (Web Site at: *http://www.ojp,usdoj.gov/bjs/abstract/ptc.htm*), the number of minor children with an imprisoned father rose 58 percent from 1991 through 1999, compared to a 98 percent increase during the same period in the number of minors with an imprisoned mother. When ministering to women in jail/prison, the primary prayer request is for their children. One of the most compelling factors in a woman ex-offender is their children's welfare.

There are many ways a women's prison ministry could minister to children. When a woman is released from prison they must obtain a home, job, and transportation for all their needs. As a parent it is almost impossible to take care of all these commitments at one time. A support group could be developed to help these women and their children become re-acquainted by offering to baby sit, go with them on inexpensive outings, and give moral support for the various difficulties relating to community re-establishment. In being there for them at this time in their re-entry into society, they will, in turn, be able to help other ex-offenders in the future. Jesus has given us a reconciliation mandate,

> *(II Corinthians 5:18-20, NKJ) "Now all things are of God, who has reconciled us to Himself through Jesus Christ and has given us the ministry of reconciliation, that is that God was in Christ reconciling the world to Himself, not imputing their trespasses to them, and has committed to us the word of reconciliation. Now then, we are ambassadors for Christ, as though God were pleading through us; we implore you on Christ's behalf, be reconciled to God."*

As we enter further into the 21st Century with the mounting evidence and staggering statistics of women's incarceration, surely the need for laborers to go into the jails/prisons is apparent as never before. This outreach isn't for everyone, but surely does qualify a cause for the "Who-so-ever-Will"!

Notes:

[1] Buell, Maureen (June 2004). *Children of Inmates.* Corrections Today

[2] Klaus, Tal & Dee (1997). *"Innovator Ministries"* Prison Ministry.

[3] Robeson, Carol & Jerry Robeson (1990), *Strongman's His Name...What's His Game?.,* Shiloh Publishing House.

[4] Re-Entry, Art Lyons, "www.reentry.org"

End of Chapter Questions

Chapter 12

1. What are the rules for ministering in prison?
2. Why is it important to assess your prison audiences, before selecting your material to be used for ministry?
3. What are the qualifications for a team member for prison ministry?
4. What are some of the guidelines for administering "deliverance" in a prison setting?
5. Write a summary indicating the value of a Re-entry Program.

Part 5

RUN TOWARD THE GOAL

"Not that I have now attained (this ideal) or have already been made perfect, but I press on to lay hold of (grasp) and make my own, that for which Christ Jesus (the Messiah) has laid hold of me and made me His own (yet); but one thing I do (it is my one aspiration), forgetting what lies behind and straining forward to what lies ahead, I <u>press on toward the goal</u> to win the (supreme and heavenly) prize to which God in Christ Jesus is calling us upward."

(Philippians 3:14, Amplified)

PART 5: Run Toward the Goal

In running the race toward a goal, you will find many obstacles along the way. These obstacles will come in many forms. They are distractions to keep you from completing your destiny in God. We know God is a God of completion; what He begins in you, He will complete.

"And I am convinced and sure of this very thing, that He Who began a good work in you, will continue until the day of Jesus Christ (right up to the time of His return), developing (that good work) and perfecting and bringing it to full completion in you."

(Philippians 1:6)

In the race that is set before us, we know that training is required. Any runner in a race will testify regarding the mental and physical stamina required to prepare to win a race. In the race set before us in the Kingdom of God, there is also spiritual stamina required. All areas encountered along the way of life will need special preparation and training. Many leaders who have attended college or university will testify of the importance of addressing the total body, soul, and spirit of mankind. A holistic view of life and ministry is essential for the equipping the saints for the work of the ministry. That is why it is so important to have 'Practical Training" while you are completing your education.

As students, study course objectives and related specifics, it is a proven fact that performance of what you have learned is a vital part of training for the ministry. If a soldier, after receiving verbal instructions and passing all the required written tests, did not have the opportunity to use what he has learned in pre-battle practical training he would be prone to receiving serious battle injuries and even death. For example, as leaders on the battlefield, if you allow doubt and fear to enter your heart, you will not be able to see yourself winning the race. It is important to develop a routine of discipline to build your endurance, once you have prepared your mind and heart to win.

Chapter 13: *Women's Ministry That Makes The Difference*

There are many books written on women of the Bible and how they ran the race the Lord set before them (*Referenced in Appendix 6*). In particular, the book *"Daughters of the Church,"* (authors Ruth A. Tucker and Walter L. Liefeld, Zondervan Publishing House, 1987), references women in ministry from the New Testament times to modern day. This is an excellent book on the history of women in the church. It starts with the gospels and the world of Jesus and ends with some notable women's ministries in the 20th century.

The role of women in the church has not received as deserving notice as men have, even when they have made outstanding contributions to the Body of Christ. Many historians have written that women represent a greater percentage of church membership than do men. Also noted, is that they seem to have the most impact on furthering the family's religious traditions that uphold the home's stability. In many situations we will find, as we see in history, women serving God with meaningful purpose and effectiveness, especially in the 21st Century. There are many we could mention, but profiled in this chapter are some well known and some lesser-known women in ministry that are running toward the goal set before them in a phenomenal and extraordinary way. We honor each for their dynamic service to God for His Kingdom.

Freda Lindsay – (Christ For The Nations)

Freda Lindsay was born in Saskatchewan, Canada and later moved to Oregon. She was converted at age 18 in a revival meeting held in Portland by the young evangelist, Gordon Lindsay. Freda married him five years later. Their marriage is a thrilling, modern-day story of miracles, travel, heartbreak, and victory. After pastorates in Billings, Montana and Ashland, Oregon, the Lindsays and their three children moved to Shreveport, Louisiana.

There they began an evangelistic association and publishing enterprise, "The Voice of Healing" in 1948. Later, the organization moved its headquarters to Dallas, Texas and changed its name to "Christ For The Nations." It has become one of the largest full gospel mission organizations in the world, reaching into 120 nations, helping to build over 11,400 native churches, distributing over 60 million books in 81 languages, helping to start 43 Bible schools worldwide, and providing scholarships for International students to attend Christ For The Nations Institute in Dallas, Texas, their first Bible school founded in 1970. In 1973 Gordon, her husband, went to be with the Lord. Upon his death, the board asked Freda to be his successor, which she fulfilled until her resignation as Chairman of the Board. While Freda is no longer directly responsible for the day-to-day operation of Christ for the Nations, she is still publisher-editor of Christ For The Nations' monthly magazine with a circulation of some 50,000. She writes "The World Prayer and Share Letter," a compilation of timely news tidbits from around the world, and her articles are very popular.

Freda celebrated her 90th birthday in April 2004 and has not retired. She continues her work in the office, as well as traveling to some of their Bible schools and other speaking engagements. When asked, "Why do you work so feverishly?" she responds, "Actually the souls won as a result of the ministry of Christ for the Nations makes me wish I had a thousand lives yet to live for the Lord." Freda has two honorary doctorates – one in 1977 from her alma mater, L.I.F.E Bible College; and one in 1987 from Oral Roberts University.

She wrote about the history of their ministry which is chronicled in her 1976 autobiography, "My Diary Secrets,, with the sequel, "Freda" following in 1984. She has since written three more books: "ABCs of Godly Living"; "A Book of Miracles"; and her latest, "The Second Wind."

For more information on Freda Lindsay call (214) 376-1711 or write Christ for the Nations, 3404 Conway, Dallas, TX 75224, Web Site www.cfni.org

Marilyn Hickey (Marilyn Hickey Ministries)
Marilyn Hickey met Wallace, a spirit-filled Nebraskan, while she was a schoolteacher and married him in 1954. Marilyn and Wallace pastored a church in Denver, Colorado which he founded in 1960. <u>*Marilyn Hickey Ministries*</u> *began from home Bible studies and has become an international organization positioned to "cover the earth with the word." During a 1976 retreat, God clarified Marilyn's call with Isaiah 11:9 "For the earth shall be full of the knowledge of the Lord as the waters cover the sea." Marilyn soon began to travel nationwide and introduced her*

renowned "Bible Encounter" – walking attendees through the Bible in three days. Even as far back as Marilyn's high school days, she considered becoming a foreign ambassador. As prophesied repeatedly, she is now an "ambassador for Christ" and has met with numerous world leaders, most recently the President of Ethiopia.

Years of intensive Bible study and powerful ministry has brought Marilyn to the attention of many Christian leaders and her overseas ministry is impacting nations. She has been to more than 95 nations carrying the life-changing message of God's love to the world. "Today with Marilyn & Sarah" (Sarah is Marilyn's daughter) broadcasts are reaching more than 280 million homes with the gospel across America and in nearly 50 countries on every major continent. The ministry's publications consist of 1,500 teaching cassettes, videotapes and CDs, with more than 100 books and booklets and a monthly teaching magazine with daily Bible devotionals.

Marilyn is the president and founder of Word to the World College located in Denver and a member of Oral Roberts University Educational Fellowship. Her ministry consists of miracle crusades, conventions, ministry training schools, and has overseas offices in the United Kingdom, South Africa and Australia. Marilyn received her BA at the University of Northern Colorado in 1953 and received an Honorary Doctor of Divinity from Oral Roberts University in 1986. Some of her latest books are "Breaking Generational Curses," "You Can Bounce Back from Your Setback," "What Every Person Wants to Know About Prayer," "Be Healed," and "Your Total Health Handbook: Body, Soul, Spirit."

For more information on Marilyn Hickey Ministries call (303) 729-1229 or write Marilyn Hickey Ministries, 8081 E Orchard Rd. Greenwood Village, CO 90111), Web Site www.marilynhickey.org

Joyce Meyer – (Joyce Meyer Ministries)
Joyce Meyes was born in 1943. She endured a sexually abusive childhood and finally left home and married the first young man that was interested. At age twenty-one she had her son and decided she could no longer tolerate her husband's infidelities and walked out of the marriage. In 1966 Joyce met David Meyer and they wed soon after and he adopted her son. Still happiness

continued to elude her and in 1976, out of frustration and desperation, she began crying out to God. God answered, and Joyce's life was never the same again. Joyce's marriage is now more than thirty-five years strong, and they are the parents of four children.. That same year Joyce began teaching the Word of God, and entered full-time ministry in 1980. As an associate pastor at Life Christian Center in St. Louis, Missouri, she coordinated and taught a weekly meeting. After five years, the Lord brought it to a conclusion, directing her to establish her own ministry, which is now called <u>Joyce Meyer Ministries</u>.

Today, her teachings are enjoyed internationally, and she travels extensively conducting conferences. Finding herself "a Christian in need of victory" many years ago, she discovered freedom to live victoriously through applying the Word. She believes that every person who walks in victory leads many others into victory. Joyce openly talks about her abuse as a child, her failed first marriage, and her struggles over the years. Her life is transparent, and her teachings are practical and can be applied in everyday life. She is an incredible testimony of the dynamic saving work of Jesus Christ and teaches that regardless of anyone's background or mistakes, God has a place for them and can help them on their path to enjoying everyday life. Her vision is in accordance with the call of God upon everyone's lives.

Joyce Meyer's God-inspired vision is to reach the world with the truth. Daily, millions of people receive life-changing biblical teaching through her television and radio programs, teaching tapes, videos, and conferences. Her television program reaches a potential audience of 2.5 billion people worldwide. Joyce is one of the world's leading teachers, spreading God's Word to billions around the globe. Joyce holds an Honorary Doctorate of Divinity degree from Oral Roberts University and a Ph.D. in Theology from Life Christian University in Tampa, Florida.. Some of her latest books are "The Secret Power of Speaking God's Word," "Battlefield of the Mind," "Managing Your Emotions," and "Me and My Big Mouth."

For more information on Joyce Myers Ministries call (636) 349-0303 or write Joyce Meyer Ministries, P.O. Box 655, Fenton, MO 63026, Web Site www.joycemeyers.org

Bishop Ernestine C. Reems (Ernestine C. Reems Ministries, Inc.)

Bishop Ernestine C. Reems has been ministering the gospel for over 30 years. With enormous faith, and little more than a dream in her heart and a vision from God, the Center of Hope Community Church was founded in 1968 with four members. Today its membership is over 1500. She established and continues her pastorate as the founder and pastor of Center of Hope Community Church in Oakland, CA. Bishop Reems shepherds one of the largest churches on the West Coast. She and the church enjoy international fame and recognition as a beacon in the community and a model for aspiring ministries everywhere.

From humble beginnings, as the third child of a family of nine, Bishop Reems learned what a life of faith in God could do. Stricken with tuberculosis at the age of thirteen, she was ill for several years. God, however, had other plans for her life. Realizing she was created for His good purpose and not her own, she determined to live for God. The Lord spared her life and her cry became, "Oh Lord, please use me, for surely there is a work that I can do."

Much of the credit for her foundation and ministry roots comes from following in the footsteps of her father, Bishop E.E. Cleveland. As a young adult, she traveled to every major city as an evangelist with her brother, Reverend Elmer Cleveland. Although women in the ministry were not readily accepted, Bishop Reems would not be denied and continues to follow her calling as a truly anointed woman of God.

The hallmark of Bishop Reems' ministry is her compelling love through Christ for people in need. Her non-judgmental attitude is one of the keys to her success in helping those considered to be outcasts to re-assimilate into society. These include recovering drug addicts, prostitutes, prisoners, ex-prisoners, the homeless, and others. In her efforts to meet the physical as well as emotional needs of others, she offers both the hope of the Gospel message and the practical demonstration of it. Working with federal, state, and local agencies as well as her congregation, Bishop Reems has raised funds to build and/or restore facilities for housing seniors, homeless single women with children, and affordable housing for other people in need.

In 1973, the United States Army requested Bishop Reems and her crusade party to go to West Germany to minister to the soldiers there. Although the Army honored her as a Five-Star General, she believes her greatest accomplishment comes as a result of her teaching and preaching the gospel that won many soldiers to Christ. In 1988, Bishop Reems organized the E.C. Reems Women's International Ministries. Under her direction and leadership, its charter is to encourage and energize women to be active partners in the gospel of the Lord and to work in their local churches.

In additional to her many ministerial duties, she is the loving mother of two sons (Brandon and Brian). Her husband of 41 years, Paul Reems, recently went home to be with the Lord. She lives in Oakland close to her church and community where her mission is to be near the people that God is using her to minister to. Bishop Reems is the author of two books, "Counting Everything As Joy," and "Through the Storm."

For more information contact Ernestine C. Reems Ministries, 20885 Redwood Road, Castro Valley, CA 94546-5915 or call (510) 562-3201, Web Site, www.bishopecreems,org/events.htm.

Dr. Beverly "BAM" Crawford (Beverly "BAM" Crawford Ministries)
Dr. Crawford is the Pastor and Founder of Beverly "BAM" Crawford Ministries, Bible Enrichment Fellowship International Church (BEFIC); Bible Enrichment Seminars, (BES); Chosen Vessels (a women's ministry); and Leaders Apostolic Mentoring Prophetic Seminars (LAMPS) conferences which are designed to provide teaching, fellowship, counseling/mentoring, and training for leaders of this generation. BEFIC was established in November 1989, after two years of community outreach, Bible seminars, leadership seminars, and national and international exposure. On any given Sunday you will experience two great forces flowing under the anointing of the Holy Spirit; the dynamic preaching of the Word of God and the prophetic ministry of praise and worship. It is in this powerful setting that the hurting are healed, the bound are set free, and those in despair receive hope to turn their lives around.

Dr. Crawford has devoted 29 years to Biblical studies and teaching. Her extensive library consists of books, and audio and video tapes, on almost every major topic in both the Old and

New Testaments. She shepherds with care, ease, excellence, and authority. Her unique prophetic teaching has helped literally thousands around the world. Dr. Crawford's commitment to the Word of God is evidenced by her discerning, yet "no-nonsense" approach to very sensitive situations. She is definitely an end-time "voice" anointed by the Holy Spirit to raise the consciousness of those who have "ears to hear" what the Spirit of God is saying.

God has placed Dr. Crawford in positions (locally and abroad) to provide some of the essentials needed to equip His people by helping them establish and maintain a strong foundation in the Word of God. Dr. Crawford serves as a Trustee on a worldwide pastor's ministerial board. God continually uses her to assist ministers in identifying their call, gifts, and offices.

The Bible Enrichment World Media Outreach consists of a radio ministry, "It's a Good Day"; a television ministry, "Bible Enrichment – The Uncompromising Word"; Internet Web Site; audio teaching tapes and videos, and music ministry albums, "The King Is Coming Any Day," recently recorded by her choir, "BAM" Crawford's Purpose." Each outreach is touching and is changing lives globally. Dr. Crawford heads a community-oriented ministry with a heart for the fallen called "Pathway." Pathway is a fellowship designed to lead people along a path to spiritual recovery over addictive and abusive behavior through prayer and the consistent application of God's Word.

In November 2004, Dr. Crawford dedicated the Kingdom Community & Youth Center (formerly the Inglewood YMCA) to the Lord. The facility will consist of community outreach programs and community development to promote social and economic change designed to benefit at-risk youth, senior citizens and small businesses.

Dr. Crawford has three children and ten grandchildren, which understandably, she says, provokes her to train and inspire this generation.

For more information contact Beverly "BAM" Crawford Ministries, 400 East Kelso Street, Inglewood, CA or call (310) 330-4700, Web Site www.bamcm.org/website.html

Carol Cartwright - (Cartwright Christian Ministries)

Carol Cartwright is an ordained minister whose life is a manifestation of the power and love of Jesus Christ. Many pastors call her Apostle, others call her Prophet, but Carol's favorite name given to her by others is "Mama Carol." She has spiritual children in many countries of the world. Her ministry travels have taken her to England, Scotland, Wales, France, Switzerland, Austria, Israel, Japan, Bahamas, Virgin Islands, Singapore, Indonesia, Mexico, and Canada. In her 35 years of ministry Carol has mentored and equipped many sons and daughters in their different callings. Apostles, Prophets, Pastors and intercessors are at their places of ministry because of her tireless hours of impartation.

Being healed by the power of God from mental illness while in her twenties, she has been given deep insight into mental healing in its various forms. She has been used of God to train members within the medical profession in bringing God's healing power to the minds of those she counsels. Psychiatrists, psychologists, psychiatric nurses, and social workers are ministering healing prayer and deliverance as a result of Carol's teaching.

Along with her husband, Bob, Carol has started numerous churches in the Southwest United States and Canada. Carol's husband, Bob, recently went home to be with the Lord. She continues to give accurate prophetic words and wisdom to the Body of Christ through the many churches she ministers in at the invitation of their pastors. She attended Christ for the Nations Institute, Dallas, TX, and received her Bachelor of Theology from Phoenix Bible College and Seminary, and a nursing degree from Northeast Louisiana School of Nursing. Carl is a licensed Clinical Counselor with the National Christian Counseling Association in Sarasota, Florida. She presently leads the Prophetic Learning Community of the Simple Church House Church Network in Texas, and is also involved in the leadership of the local church within the House Church Network. Carol is well known for her extensive labor in Canada for the last 22 years.

When God told her to go north to Canada, and especially to Vancouver, little did she know that years later she would still be ministering there and that through her ministry many souls would be won to the kingdom of God. Carol has written "Beginning Ministries Manual," and "Doctrines of Satan and Demons."

For more information contact Cartwright Christian Ministries, P.O. Box 3488, Cedar Hill, TX, 75106, or call (972) 299-6861. Web Site www.cartwrightchrisitanministries.org.

Dr. Kluane Spake *(Sword Ministries)*

Dr. Spake founded and pastored for 14 years Jubilee Church, a multi-cultural and multi-ethnic church on the island of Guam. She remains president of that church. She also supervised a network of churches in the Philippines. She now travels full time as a conference speaker, Bible college teacher, also holds foreign crusades, pastor's conventions, and ministers to thousands in Asia, India, the United States, and many other nations of the world. She has successfully planted local churches, raising up leaders, and impacting entire communities with the gospel of the Lord Jesus Christ. She is dedicated to helping Christians tap into their enormous potential and increase their sense of direction, confidence, and ability to operate in the supernatural.

Dr. Spake imparts revelation knowledge and presents truth which is impacting the current Apostolic Movement within the Body of Christ. She is considered a pioneer in the preaching on "the finished work of redemption" that enables believers to become fully whole in this lifetime. Dr. Spake has worked with hundreds of churches worldwide. She speaks from the heart, which touches people individually and has a way of making the seemingly complex easy to understand. Her passion in the ministry is to provide accurate Biblical understanding that will cause believers to shed preconceived religious notions, and press into a powerful comprehension of the infallible Word of God. As a highly focused preacher, author, speaker, coach and consultant, she is highly esteemed in the arena of preaching on the deep revelations of scripture. Called by her peers the "Apostle of Women," Dr. Spake has a strong educational background with a Masters degree from Trinity Theological Seminary and a Doctorate in Theology from Vision International College & University. She is listed in "Who's Who in the World," and "Who's Who in America." She is an author of many books and her best well-known books are "Enmity to Equality, and "Whole and Holy." She also wrote an exciting, interactive, and professional children's curriculum called "Angel's Friends." She is a member of the International Coalition of Apostles. Dr. Spake's family lives near Atlanta, Georgia.

For more information contract Sword Ministries, P.O. Box 941933, Atlanta, GA 31141, or call (678) 584-0711, or E-mail Spake@mindspring,com; Web Site www.kluane.org.

Dr. Patricia Hulsey (Harvestime International)

Dr. Hulsey is a co-founder of Harvestime International Network with her husband, Rev. Argis Hulsey. It was birthed in 1983 to fill a great need she had noted in her international travels. The cry coming from the nations of the world was for materials specifically designed to help national Christian leaders reach their own people with the Gospel and then train them to be reproductive believers reaching out to others. As the ministry began to search for such materials, she found much of the existing literature poorly written for the average layman in Third World nations. She also discovered problems with translation and reproduction rights, making most materials unavailable for the nations. God put it on her heart to begin writing a few courses for a few friends overseas. As she did so, they ran copies off on copy machines, and used them. These few friends told others, and the ministry of Harvestime was birthed as it multiplied round the world.

Harvestime now reaches nations all around the world through their distribution of printed materials, CD ROMS, and through their Web Site. Their Asian Internet Bible School has 4,000 on-line students. All of the courses are available in Russian, Spanish, Thai, and Portuguese. Harvestime is not in competition with the traditional Bible College structure. The ministry is for laymen and women who do not have the opportunity for such training because of geographical location, finances, or educational issues. Harvestime International Network is a member of the Vision International Education Network.

Harvestime has been in the prison ministry for 14 years, the two largest facilities being Chowchilla and Valley State Prison located in California. Dr. Hulsey has ministered to the general population, filled in for Chaplains, and ministered in California death row for women inmates. She developed a manual on jail/prison ministry that is being used around the world to raise up prison ministries and train prison workers. The facilities download all her material free of charge. Dr. Hulsey developed the "Harvestime International Prison Institute," whose purpose is to raise up fully functional churches within the prison system; churches that not only recognize their responsibility to reach the prison but the entire world with the Gospel of Christ. The inmates can receive college credits for their Harvestime courses which may be transferred to a four-year institute for a Bachelors degree if desired (through partnership with Vision International College and University, www.vision.edu) Dr. Hulsey received her Masters Degree in School Administration from Western Graduate School and her Doctorate in Philosophy from Trinity Theological Seminary. She served on the faculty of Trinity Theological Seminary, Global Bible Institute, and Vision International College and University. She has ministered in seminars, churches, and prisons around the world and traveled to 45 nations of the world. From 1978-1982 she was the Executive assistant to Evangelist Morris Cerullo, World Evangelism and still does free-lance projects for Dr. Cerullo. She authored and published more than 25 books, including the entire Harvestime International Network training series.

For more information contact Harvestime International Network, 14431 Tierra Drive, Colorado Springs, CO 80921, or call (719) 487-3265 Web Site www.harvestime.org.

Cindy Jacobs - (Generals of Intercession)

Widely recognized as a prophet to the nations, Dr. Cindy Jacobs is the President and Co-Founder of Generals of Intercession, a missionary organization devoted to training in prayer and spiritual warfare. Cindy's call to prophetic intercession was made clear to her during an extended season of seeking God's face when she was 20 years old. She found herself praying with detailed accuracy over situations and people as the Holy Spirit took hold of burdens and brought forth blessings. This prophetic gift was honed in the prayer closet long before stepping into public ministry. Intercession is a training ground for the prophetic gifts.

In 1985, Cindy and her husband Mike founded Generals of Intercession, with the intention of developing prayer strategies to unlock a harvest in the nations of the world. From the foundation of the ministry, God emphasized the need to "gather the gatekeepers" in cities, regions, and nations to receive together a corporate strategy for revival. Cindy ministers in conferences throughout the world, embracing the Father's promise in Psalm 2:8, "Ask of Me and I will give you the nations as your inheritance and the uttermost parts of the earth for your possessions." A major focus of her ministry in this regard is mobilizing strategic intercession to tear down strongholds that blind the masses to Jesus Christ.

In addition to speaking engagements, Cindy also shares on strategic global prayer thrusts in the bi-annual publication, the GI News. In 1996, Cindy was asked by C. Peter Wagner to coordinate the Spiritual Warfare Network for the United States. Since then, Cindy has established state coordinators throughout the nation to help mobilize strategic level intercession. An ordained minister, in 1999 Cindy was granted an honorary Doctorate of Divinity from the Christian International Seminary in Florida, founded by Bishop Bill Hamon.

In the spring of 2000, Thomas Nelson Publishers released the new Women of Destiny Study Bible, which was edited by Cindy and features contributions from women in leadership throughout the body of Christ. She is an author of three best-selling books, including "Possessing the Gates of the Enemy," "The Voice of God," and "Deliver Us From Evil." The global headquarters for Generals of Intercession is located at Red Oak, Texas.

For more information on Cindy Jacobs call (972) 576-8887 or write Generals of Intercession, P.O. 340, Red Oak, Texas, 75154, Web Site www.Generals.org.

Paula White (Paula White Ministries)
Pastor Paula White, along with husband Randy, are pastors of Without Walls International Church in Tampa, Florida, a congregation of nearly 15,000 members. She is also head of the Paula White Ministries and host of a daily TV show, Paula White Today, and has a biweekly radio program.

When God moved their ministry from Washington, DC to Tampa FL in 1990, God laid on their hearts an incredible vision for broken and hurting children and youth. Their church was birthed in 1991 with a heart and call for evangelism and restoration. Part of their mandate was not only to impact their city, but also to train and equip leadership around the nation and the world to make a difference in their cities. Through this vision they have trained tens of thousands of people and ministries since 1994 through Operation Explosion International Training Center held quarterly. They have since developed and overseen more than 200 ministries that serve the needs of both the church body and the community. As a symbol of their growth and desire to impact every person for Jesus Christ, they unveiled their new name in 1997, Without Walls International Church.

On the personal side, God had a perfect plan designed for Pastor Paula even through her childhood of suffering both physical and sexual abuse, which resulted in bouts of depression, low self-esteem and self-worth. She did not hear the traditional message of the Gospel until she was eighteen years old. In the midst of everything that she encountered, God wanted to use what the enemy meant for evil and turn it around for her good. God had a plan and she knows that she was created with purpose and destiny. She says God wants to turn our stumbling blocks into stepping stones. Their ministry has won over one million souls to the Kingdom. She quotes, "Who would have thought that a little messed-up Mississippi girl who was overwhelmed and just simple, would be used of God? God did and He turned my pain into power and I went from being a victim to living victoriously."

Paula White Ministries is being used to touch many women's lives, helping them through God to develop their full potential and purpose. She has authored many books and her most recent books are "He Loves Me, He Loves Me Not," and "Deal With It."

For more information contact Paula White Ministries, P.O. Box 25151, Tampa, Florida, 33622, or call (813) 879-4673 Web Site www.paulawhite.org.

Epilogue

As I began in the prologue, my desire was to write a women's ministry book that was a collection of experiences and the many materials used to prepare women for effective ministry. I had initially determined that there was a limited amount of material in regards to this subject matter. As I continued to research and write, I found there are indeed many books and articles on various aspects of women's ministry which have contributed to the subject matter for this text. In fact, sources were much more plentiful than I was able to include in this book. My hope has been to condense the most important material so as to do justice to the wealth of knowledge available.

The primary goal of this text was stressed at the beginning to provide the nitty-gritty of planning, developing, and implementing a ministry to reach the non-Christian women and to disciple, develop and encourage Christian women in your particular circle of influence.

More, perhaps, could have been included about spiritual development or discipleship, but there is a abundance of good books available by many ministries that enhance our spiritual growth in all areas. Much more could have been included in the many outreach opportunities available for women and how to implement them. For example, this would include outreaches to hospital patients, hospice assistance, shut-ins, senior care homes, etc. Other "outreaches" not discussed, but which can be part of the local church body include food and clothing distribution, wedding planning, altar ministry, prayer groups, etc. The numbers of opportunities are endless, but with prayer, hearing from God, planning, and proper implementation, these opportunities can be turned into fruitful service for our King.

In closing, further comments on an area not mentioned previously are needed. I have encountered the many struggles of working women who are followers of Christ in the workplace. In spite of problems, they have been able to fulfill their anointed calling in the Lord and have been a great testimony and inspiration to women's ministry.

Women face challenging problems in responding to the priorities of their faith, family, ministry, and the workplace. In meeting women who have successfully integrated this challenge, I have found some common elements among them.

- Hearing God's calling is essential, and walking in the anointing is vital. To do so you must be close to the heart of God to hear his voice.
- Total dependence on God is necessary, praying for His guidance in every situation.
- Rational and authentic interaction with co-workers who are difficult is difficult. We need to be an advocate of servant-leadership, with Jesus as our primary model.
- Biblical ethics in daily work is mandatory.
- A woman must be confident that she has properly balanced career and family, so she can minister with confidence and freedom without conflict.

These working women have been a great inspiration for me. Professional women as leaders in their field have found ways to promote their belief in God within their career.

In today's world, whether we have been called to be a housewife, professional, or lay person in ministry, we need to ensure the same balance shown above. God can help us to face obstacles we may encounter, whether in business or in our personal lives. The formula is the same, Christ is our model and God has uniquely gifted us to bring Christ to daily experience. No matter how big or impossible it may seem, there is no limit to what God will do. He is waiting for us to accept the call!

APPENDICES

Appendix	Title	Page
1	Sample Brochure for Women's Ministry	225
2	Motivational Gifts Test	227
3	Sample Brochure for Conference/Retreat	235
4	Sample Conference/Retreat Timeline	237
5	Sample Conference/Retreat Budget	239
6	Recommended Reading for Women's Ministry	241

APPENDIX 1   SAMPLE BROCHURE FOR WOMEN'S MINISTRY

Vision

The vision of Women of Destiny Ministry is to seek to fulfill Christ's mission by encouraging women with a sense of belonging to God and each other, enabling women in becoming all they are to be in Christ, and equipping women for blessing others with the love, grace, and truth of Jesus Christ to meet the complex needs of today's women.

"Each one has received a special gift, employ it in serving one another, as good stewards of the manifold grace of God. Whoever speaks, let him speak, as it were, the utterance of God; whoever serves, let him do so as by the strength which God supplies; so that in all things God may be glorified through Jesus Christ, to whom belongs the glory and dominion forever and ever."
(I Peter 4:10)

Purpose

- To help produce the will of God in the lives of women.

- To maximize the potential and revelation that God has for her destiny.

- To train spiritual leaders to reach out to women, to bring them hope, healing, and reconciliation to God in a world that is crying out for help.

- To build God's influence in her life to be able to touch her home and family in a changing society with so many distractions from God's purpose of the family unit.

- To recognize and support the unity of the Spirit in the Body of Christ, so the world can know we are His disciples.

Our Goal

"As women grow and mature in godliness, that they will be better equipped to nurture and serve in their families, to enrich the church body, to evangelize their communities and for those called, to be sent out to evangelize in other parts of our nation and world"

Ministry

Listed below are the types of ministry we offer:

- Monthly Meetings
- Weekly Bible Studies
- Support Groups
  - Substance Abuse
  - Co-Dependency
- Hospital Visits
- Prison Ministry
- Pastoral Counseling
- Seminar Classes:
  - Parenting
  - Christian Life
  - Evangelism
  - Family Violence
- Yearly Conference/Retreat

We look forward to you joining us and participating in one of our outreach ministries.

For more information please call the office and someone will return your call: (AAA) XXX-YYYY

Women of Destiny Ministry

Leading Women
To New Heights
Toward Their Destiny

Jesus said: *"Go make disciples"*
Matthew 28:19

Located at:
Some Street
Your City, ST 12345

Telephone (AAA) XXX-YYYY
Fax: (AAA) XXX-ZZZZ

Ministry Hours:
Mon – Thurs., 8am –4:00pm

Ministry Beliefs
We Believe…

There is only one God.
(John 17:3)

The Bible is the inspired word of God
(II Timothy 3:17:3)

In the Triune nature of the Godhead;
God the Father, God the Son, and God the Holy Spirit
(I Peter 1:2 & Matthew 18:19)

It is important that a Christian receive the in-filling of the Holy Spirit
(Acts 2:4, 38 & 39)

In the present day operation of the gifts of the Holy Spirit
((I Corinthians 12)

In the present day ministry of the five fold gifts
(Ephesians 4:9-14)

The Run for the Goal
"Write the vision, and make it plain upon tables, that he may run that read it"
(Habakkuk 2:2)

Women of Destiny Ministry is intended as an enhancement for women – whether they are just checking out Christianity, have newly accepted Christ as Savior, or are already richly grounded through the Word of God.

Purpose Statement

- *To worship Christ, serve Him, and fellowship.*

- *To grow like Him in character and to fulfill our mission in the world.*

- *To be a member of Christ's family, a messenger of His Word and to bring Him glory.*

APPENDIX 2   MOTIVATIONAL GIFTS TEST

IDENTIFYING YOUR MOTIVATIONAL GIFTS
(Dr. Jason & Pastor Cathy Guerrero)

KEY: **+ (Usually characterizes me)**
    MID (Sometimes characterizes me)
        - (Hardly ever characterizes me)

1. I have the ability to recall specific likes and dislikes of people.
2. I have the ability to make wise purchases and investments.
3. When another person is having problems I have the desire to see what needs to be done and prescribe steps of action.
4. I have the ability to feel an atmosphere of joy or distress in an individual or group.
5. I have the alertness to detect and meet practical needs. I especially enjoy manual projects.
6. I have a desire to give money quietly to effective projects or ministries. (Avoiding pressure of publicity)
7. I have a tendency to avoid telling people information which lacks practical application to their lives.
8. I have an attraction to and an understanding of people who are in distress.
9. I have the motivation to meet needs as quickly as possible.
10. I attempt to use my giving to motivate others to give.
11. I have the ability to see how troubles can produce new levels of maturity.
12. I have a desire to remove hurts and bring healing to others.
13. I have the physical stamina to fulfill others' needs with disregard for weariness.
14. I have an alertness to point out monetary needs which others might overlook.
15. I have a greater concern for mental distress than physical distress.
16. I have the willingness to use personal funds to avoid delays.
17. I have an enjoyment in meeting needs without the pressure of appeals.
18. I especially like to discover insights from human experience which can be validated and amplified in Scripture.
19. I avoid firmness unless I see how it will bring benefit.
20. I have the desire to sense sincere appreciation and the ability to detect insincerity.
21. I have special joy when my money is an answer to specific prayer.
22. I have enjoyment with those eager to follow steps of action.
23. I have a sensitivity to words and actions which will hurt other people.
24. I believe it is necessary to counsel with my husband/wife to confirm the amount of a gift.
25. I have grief when teaching is not accompanied by practical steps of action.
26. I have the ability to discern sincere motives in other people.
27. I have an involvement in a variety of activities and find it difficult to say "no."
28. I have a concern that my monetary giving be of high quality.
29. I have a delight in personal conferences with others that result in new insights for them.
30. I have a greater enjoyment of short-range goals with frustration over long-range goals.

31. I have a desire to feel a part of the work or person to whom I give money.
32. I have an enjoyment and unity with those who are sensitive to the needs and feelings of others.
33. I have a frustration when limitations of time are attached to jobs.
34. I do not feel close in spirit to those who are insincere or insensitive.
35. I have a need to express my message verbally.
36. I have an ability to see the overall picture and to clarify long-range goals.
37. I have the belief that the gift of teaching is foundational to other gifts.
38. I have the ability to discern the character and motives of people.
39. I have the motivation to organize that for which I am responsible.
40. I have an emphasis on the accuracy of words.
41. I have the capacity to identify, define, and hate evil.
42. I have the desire to complete tasks as quickly as possible.
43. I like to test the knowledge of those who are teaching me.
44. I have a willingness to experience brokenness to prompt brokenness.
45. I have an awareness of the resources available to complete a task.
46. I delight in research in order to validate biblical truth.
47. I depend on Scriptural truth to validate my authority.
48. I have the ability to know what can or cannot be delegated.
49. I have a desire to see outward evidences to demonstrate inward conviction.
50. I have a tendency to stand on the sidelines until those in charge turn over responsibility to me.
51. I like to present Biblical and theological truth in a systematic sequence.
52. I have a directness, frankness, and persuasiveness in speaking.
53. I have the tendency to assume responsibility if no structured leadership exists.
54. I try to avoid illustrations from non-Biblical sources.
55. I have a deep concern for the reputation and program of God.
56. I have the willingness to endure reaction from workers in order to accomplish the ultimate task.
57. I have a special sensitivity and resistance to Scriptural illustrations out of context.
58. I have an inward weeping and personal identification with the sins of those I talk with.
59. I have great fulfillment in seeing all the pieces coming together and others enjoying the finished product.
60. I have a greater joy in doing detailed research of Biblical truth than in presenting it.
61. I have an eagerness to help other people see their personal blind spots.
62. I have a desire to move on to a new challenge when a previous task is fully completed.
63. I especially like to see that people are paying attention when I am speaking to them.
64. I have the desire to complete a job with evidence of unexpected extra service.
65. I have the ability to verify new truths by established principles of Biblical truth.

ADDITIONAL QUESTIONS TO DISCERN YOUR SPIRITUAL GIFT IF YOU HAVE NARROWED DOWN YOUR MOTIVATIONAL GIFT TO TWO OR THREE, THE FOLLOWING QUESTIONS MAY ASSIST YOU TO DISCERN YOUR BASIC MOTIVATION.

66. If you were limited to either doing research for a lesson or presenting that lesson, which would you choose?
   A. Research
   B. Presenting Lesson
67. Do you enjoy research in order to present that which you have learned or in order to clarify and prove that which has been taught?
   A. Present
   B. Clarify and Prove

Prophecy or Teaching
68. Do you enjoy speaking more to a group or to an individual?
   A. Group
   B. Individual
69. When speaking to a group do you receive greater joy from seeing an immediate response of commitment or do you enjoy the opportunity to counsel as a result or speaking?
   A. Response of Commitment
   B. Counsel
70. Do you enjoy personal follow-up to encourage spiritual growth or in order to confirm and strengthen the commitment that a person has made?
   A. Encourage Spiritual Growth
   B. Confirm Commitment

Serving or Mercy
71. Are you more comfortable in helping to meet the practical needs of others or in meeting their mental and emotional needs?
   A. Practical Needs
   B. Emotional Needs

Teaching or Mercy
72. Are you more concerned with the atmosphere of a worship service or the Scriptural pattern of a worship service?
   A. Atmosphere
   B. Scriptural Pattern

Serving or Ruling
73. If you were given the responsibility to organize for an activity, would you prefer delegating the responsibilities to others or perform most of the responsibilities yourself?
   A. Delegate
   B. Perform by Self
74. Which do you enjoy most, short-range projects or long-range projects?
   A. Short-Range
   B. Long-Range

Serving or Exhortation

75. Do you enjoy counseling an individual in order to give them steps or action or in order to discern what their practical needs are and how to meet their needs?
    A. Steps of Action
    B. Meet Practical Needs

76. In helping a person with a problem would you be more comfortable in counseling them or in meeting a practical need?
    A. Counseling
    B. Meet Practical Needs

77. Do you enjoy teaching in order to participate in research or as an opportunity to counsel others?
    A. Research
    B. Counsel

78. In finding solutions to human problems, do you usually begin with Scripture and relate them to human experiences or do you usually begin with human experiences and relate them to Scripture?
    A. Scripture and Human Experience
    B: Experience and Scripture

Exhortation or Ruling

79. If you were responsible for an organization where conflicts were caused by an employee, would you have the tendency to change the employee's responsibilities and position or would you focus on designing steps to solve the conflict.
    A. Change Responsibilities
    B. Solve the Conflict

Giving or Serving

80. Do you receive greater joy in giving to meet the practical needs of an individual or in giving to a person who is involved in a specific ministry to others?
    A. Meet Practical Needs
    B. Person Involved in a Ministry

Exhortation or Mercy

81. Are you interested in healing for the sake of preventing unnecessary suffering or that through healing you may challenge one on to spiritual maturity?
    A. Healing to Prevent Unnecessary Suffering
    B. Healing to Challenge Spiritual Growth

82. Are you interested in spiritual growth primarily for the sake of maturity or by growing spiritually one may eliminate suffering and disharmony caused by wrong responses?
    A. Growth for Maturity
    B. Growth to Eliminate Disharmony

83. Which is more important, that you are able to sense a genuine concern and interest in a person helping you or that the person can give you steps of action in solving a problem?
    A. Genuine Concern
    B. Steps of Action

Ruling or Mercy

84. Do you desire harmony in an organization in order that it may run smoothly or because of the joy and fellowship which results?
    A. Run Smoothly
    B. Joy and Fellowship

85. Do you receive greater joy in being able to openly and freely discuss a problem or designing steps to solve the problem?
    A. Discuss Problem
    B. Solve Problem

Mercy or Teaching

86. Are you motivated to do research in order to establish correct doctrine or in order to understand doctrinal differences among Christians and how to bring harmony and oneness?
    A. Correct Doctrine
    B. Harmony and Oneness

SCORE SHEET FOR SPIRITUAL GIFT SURVEY

1.	+	mid	-	44.	+	mid	-	66.	A___ B.___
2.	+	mid	-	45.	+	mid	-	67.	A___ B.___
3.	+	mid	-	46.	+	mid	-	68.	A___ B.___
4.	+	mid	-	47.	+	mid	-	69.	A___ B.___
5.	+	mid	-	48.	+	mid	-	70.	A___ B.___
6.	+	mid	-	49.	+	mid	-	71.	A___ B.___
7.	+	mid	-	50.	+	mid	-	72.	A___ B.___
8.	+	mid	-	51.	+	mid	-	73.	A___ B.___
9.	+	mid	-	52.	+	mid	-	74.	A___ B.___
10.	+	mid	-	53.	+	mid	-	75.	A___ B.___
11.	+	mid	-	54.	+	mid	-	76.	A___ B.___
12.	+	mid	-	55.	+	mid	-	77.	A___ B.___
13.	+	mid	-	56.	+	mid	-	78.	A___ B.___
14.	+	mid	-	57.	+	mid	-	79.	A___ B.___
15.	+	mid	-	58.	+	mid	-	80.	A___ B.___
16.	+	mid	-	59.	+	mid	-	81.	A___ B.___
17.	+	mid	-	60.	+	mid	-	82.	A___ B.___
18.	+	mid	-	61.	+	mid	-	83.	A___ B.___
19.	+	mid	-	62.	+	mid	-	84.	A___ B.___
20.	+	mid	-	63.	+	mid	-	85.	A___ B.___
21.	+	mid	-	64.	+	mid	-	86.	A___ B.___
22.	+	mid	-	65.	+	mid	-		
23.	+	mid	-						
24.	+	mid	-						
25.	+	mid	-						
26.	+	mid	-						
27.	+	mid	-						
28.	+	mid	-						
29.	+	mid	-						
30.	+	mid	-						
31.	+	mid	-						
32.	+	mid	-						
33.	+	mid	-						
34.	+	mid	-						
35.	+	mid	-						
36.	+	mid	-						
37.	+	mid	-						
38.	+	mid	-						
39.	+	mid	-						
40.	+	mid	-						
41.	+	mid	-						
42.	+	mid	-						
43.	+	mid	-						

TALLY SHEET FOR SPIRITUAL GIFT SURVEY

Take the answers from the answer sheet and write the response next to the appropriate question number.

Questions 1 - 64: 2 points for +
                          1 point for mid
                          0 points for -

Questions 66 - 86 2 points for check
                          0 points for non-check

SERVING	GIVING	EXHORTATION	MERCY	PROPHECY	RULING	TEACHING
1___	2___	3___	4___	38___	36___	37___
5___	6___	7___	8___	41___	39___	40___
9___	10___	11___	12___	44___	42___	43___
13___	14___	18___	15___	47___	45___	46___
16___	17___	22___	19___	49___	48___	51___
20___	21___	25___	23___	52___	50___	54___
27___	24___	29___	26___	55___	53___	57___
30___	28___	63___	32___	58___	56___	60___
33___	31___	68b___	34___	61___	59___	65___
64___	80b___	69b___	71b___	66b___	62___	66a___
71a___		70a___	72a___	67a___	73a___	67b___
73a___		75a___	81a___	68a___	74b___	72b___
74a___		76a___	82a___	69a___	79a___	77a___
75b___		77b___	83a___	70b___	84a___	78a___
76b___		78b___	84b___		85b___	86a___
80a___		79b___	85a___			
		81b___	86b___			
		82b___				
		83b___				
TOTAL	TOTAL	TOTAL	TOTAL	TOTAL	TOTAL	TOTAL
___	___	___	___	___	___	___
%___	%___	%___	%___	%___	%___	%___

APPENDIX 3: SAMPLE BROCHURE FOR CONFERENCE/RETREAT

CATALINA ISLAND

Not Just an Island – Another World

[Map of the area to get to the Retreat]

LOCATION: "Destination Catalina Island" From Dana Point (San Diego County) take the I-5 Fwy North and exit at Beach Cities Hwy #1 off ramp. Turn left at the 2nd signal, Dana Point Harbor Drive, then left at Golden Lantern, which dead ends at Dana Harbor parking lot. Take the Catalina Cruise Flyer from Dana Point at 5:00pm Friday, June 4th. Arrives at Catalina Island 6:30pm. A Shuttle will be there to pick up and escort you to the Hotel Atwater located on Sumner Ave. (one block from the beach). A greeter will meet you at the Hotel Atwater to assist you upon your arrival.

For more information contact: Pastor Dee

ADVANCE REGISTRATION REQUIRED
LIMITED SPACE AVAILABLE

Registration begins Friday, June 4, at 6:30. The retreat begins at 7:30 on Friday, meeting in lobby of the Hotel Atwater and going to Catalina Island Beach, and closes on Sunday, June 6 at the Catalina Island Beach at 11:00am. The weekend includes two Continental Breakfasts & Saturday night dinner at Channel House Restaurant.

RETREAT HIGHLIGHTS

Pastor Jane Doe –
"Reflecting His Light Through Love"
Pastor Dee Johnson –
"Guarding Your Light with Care:
Elder Wren Bonne
"A Hand of Light Extended"

Workshops/Panels
"Reflections of Women in the Bible"
Pastor Jane Doe
Gayle Ridder
Cheryl Grant
Sheri Dailey

"Reflections of Women in 21st Century"
Pastor Jane Doe
Pastor Dee Johnson
Jana Williams
Amanda White

Prayer Counselor Coordinator
"Prayer Walk & Intercessors"
Tracy Thompson

REGISTRATION FORM (Please Print)

NAME_____

ADDRESS_____

CITY/STATE_____

ZIP_____ PHONE_____

I want to room with (4 to a room)
_____
_____

(Age limit: 18 years and older)

PLEASE CHECK APPROPRIATE BOX:
{ } I am enclosing full payment of $111 $_____
    to be received by May 4, 2004
{ } I am enclosing an extra donation of $_____
    Total Enclosed $_____

CANCELLATION DEADLINE May 4, 2004. Thereafter, money will be considered as a donation to Women of Destiny, or you may transfer it to someone else if you send a written authorization and let us know.

PLEASE MAKE CHECKS PAYABLE TO:
YOUR CHRISTIAN CHURCH
Give application and check to Pastor Dee or Jodi

Your Christian Church
Return Address
City, ST, ZIP

STAMP

Mail To
Address
City, ST, ZIP

Women of Destiny

2004 Conference

June 4-6

Destination

Catalina Island

"Let your light so shine before men, that they may see your good works and glorify your Father in heaven." (Matthew 5:16)

L – *Light is contagious!*

One candle quenches the darkness. Clustered together, they brighten a room. Massed together, they have the power to light up a city, a nation, the world.

I – *It inspires us to live!*

Shrouded in darkness, the earth was once empty of life. With light, comes everything created to live, to grow. We reach out for light, inspired by the One who spoke it into being.

G – *It glows!*

Light takes on a countenance of its own that changes everything in its radiant sphere. We are drawn toward the circle with a yearning to be part of that radiance.

H – *It heats!*

The heat from a single candle can thaw chilled hands. A bonfire warms everyone in the circle.

T – *It transforms us!*

That is why the Apostle Paul said. "For you were once in darkness, but now you are light in the Lord."

APPENDIX 4 SAMPLE CONFERENCE/RETREAT TIMELINE

APPENDIX 4: SAMPLE CONFERENCE / RETREAT TIMELINE

Months	12	11	10	9	8	7	6	5	4	3	2	1	Event
Leader(s)	Meet/Plan		Meet/Plan		Meet/Plan		Meet/Plan		Meet/Plan		Meet/Plan	Meet/Finalize	
Prayer	* Meet Regularly	*	*	*	*	*	*	*	*	*	*	*	
Budget	Determine			Adjust			Review/Resources		Review/Budget		Budget/Finalize		
Theme	Determine		Select	Finalize									
Location Date	Select		Finalize										
Speaker(s)	Suggest/Contacts			Finalize				Finalize			Contact		
Workshops	Suggest/Contact		Select Presenters	Finalize								Meet/Review	
Worship Team											Contact		
Committee Chairwomen	Select	Meet	Input Budgets		Approve Budget		** Meet Regularly	**	**	**	**	**	
Reservation Committee		Meet		Submit Attendees Count	Approve/Print		Add-On Attendees			Late Add-ons		Final Count	
Brochure		Meet/Plan						Finalize	Brochure Distribute				
Decorations			Select	Select						Finalize			
Packets								Planning	Select			Complete Packet	
Counseling/Altar Min.		Meet Select						Meet/Pray		Meet/Pray		Meet/Pray	
Greeters					Train			Meet/Select	Train				
Audio/Visual										Select	Meet/Pray	Finalize	
Publicity					Meet/Plan		Decide Methods		*** Begin Publicity	***	***	***	

237

APPENDIX 5: SAMPLE CONFERENCE/RETREAT BUDGET

(Based on 100 Women)

<u>Conference/Retreat Expenses</u> Location: Catalina Island

- Catalina Flyer (Ship)
  (From – Dana Point, CA/ To – Catalina Island)
  @ $37.00 per person (Round Trip) — $3700.00
- Atwater Hotel
  (2 nights – 3 persons per room)
  @ $83.00/person. (Includes 2 Breakfast,/light lunch) — 8300.00
- Channel House Restaurant
  (Saturday night dinner)
  @ $10.26 (includes tax/gratuity) — 1026.00
- Conference Room & Workshop Rooms — 200.00
- Materials:
  - Flyers/Brochures (printed) — 50.00
  - Name Tags (with plastic covers) — 26.00
  - Packets (includes all handouts/agenda) — 160.00
  - Misc. (tissues, first aid kit, lotions, etc.) — 70.00
- Hospitality
  - Misc. Snacks (includes cups, plates, napkins) — 175.00
- Public Relations
  - Advertisement — 135.00
  - Mail out (postage) — 45.00
  - Misc. Publicity — 85.00
  - Photos (event memories) — 58.00
- Decorations
  - Meeting/Workshop Rooms (posters, plants, flowers) — 160.00
- Honorariums
  - Key Speaker (2 sessions) — 800.00
  - Workshop Teachers (5@ $100- 1 workshop each) — 500.00
  - Worship Team (3@ $75 – 3 sessions) — <u>225.00</u>

  Total Expenses — $15715.00

<u>Conference/Retreat Income</u>

- Women's Ministry Budget (Previous Balance) — 1500.00
- Fundraisers
  - Bake Sale — 550.00
  - Cook Book Sales — 875.00
- Conference Offerings — 1050.00
- Conference/Retreat Income (100 persons @ $120) — <u>12000.00</u>

  Total Income — $15975.00

<u>Balance Forward : Women's Ministry</u> — $ 260.00

APPENDIX 6: RECOMMENDED READING FOR WOMEN'S MINISTRY

BOOKS

Adams, Cris. Women Reaching Women, Beginning & Building a Growing Women's Enrichment Ministry. Life Way Press.

Alves, Elizabeth. Becoming a Prayer Warrior. Renew Books, Ventura, CA, 1998. Bilezikian, Gilbert. Beyond Sex Roles. Baker Book House.

Briscoe, Jill. Renewal on the Run. Harold Shaw Publishers.

Briscoe, Jill, McIntyre & Seversen. Designing Effective Women's Ministries. Zondervan Publishing House.

Brown, Judy. Women Ministers, According to Scripture. Morris Publishing

Bushnell, Katherine. God's Word To Women.

Chapman, Annie, and Rank, Maureen, Smart Women Keep It Simple. Bethany House Publishers, Minneapolis, MN

Clouse B. & R. Women in Ministry , Four Views of. Inter Varsity Press.

Damazio, Frank, The Making of a Leader, City Bible Publishing, 1988

Damon, Roberta McBride. Relationship Skills. Women's Missionary Union, SBC.

Deen, Edith. All the Women of the Bible. Harper Collins Publishing.

DeKoven, Stan, PhD. Journey to Wholeness. Vision Publishing.

Evans, Debra Woman of Courage. Zondervan Publishing House, 1999

Fisher, Martha, Becoming One Flesh. Fairmont Books.

Grenz, Stanley. Women of the Church. Intervarsity Press.

Grootus, Rebecca M. Good News for Women, A Biblical Picture of Gender Equality. Baker Books Publishing.

Foh, Susan. Women & The Word Of God: Response To Biblical Feminism. Reformed Publishing Co., 1997.

Hagin, Kenneth E. The Woman Question. Kenneth Hagin Ministries.

Hulsey, Patricia. Women: A Biblical Profile. Vision Publishing.

Hunter, Brenda, In the Company of Woman. Multnomah Books.

Hyatt, Suysan C., In the Spirit We're Equal, Hyatt Press

Jacobs, Cindy, Deliverance From Evil, Regal Books, Ventura, CA.

Jakes, T.D. Woman Thou Art Loosed. Destiny Image Publishers, Inc.

Jammeu, Rebecca Price. Great Women in American History. Horizon Books

Jepsen, Dee. Women Beyond Equal Rights. Word Books Publishing.

Jewett, Paul K. Man as Male and Female. William B. Eerdmans Publishing Company.

Kraft, Vickie. Women Mentoring Women, Ways to Start, Maintain & Expand a Biblical Women's Ministry. Moody Press.

Kurko, Virginia. Women Where Are Thine Accusers? Vision Publishing.

Kuyper, Abraham. Women of the New Testament. Zondervan Publishing.

Littauer, Florence. Personality Plus. Revell Publishing.

London, H.B./Wiseman, Neil. Married to a Pastor's Wife. Victor Books.

Macartney, Clarence E. Great Women of the Bible. Kregel Publishing.

Malcolm, Kari Torjesen. Women at the Crossroads. Intervarsity Press.

Malmin, Glenda. Woman You Are Called And Anointed. City Bible Publishing, Portland, OR, 1998.

Maxwell, John. Developing the Leaders Around You. Nelson Publishing.

Maxwell, John. The 17 Indisputable Laws of Teamwork, Thomas Nelson Publishers, 2001.

Maxwell, John. The 21 Irrefutable Laws of Leadership, Thomas Nelson Publishers, 1998

Mickelsen, Alvera. Women, Authority and the Bible. Intervarsity Press.

Morgan, Marabel. The Total Woman. Revel Publishing Company.

Noren C. Women in the Pulpit. Abingdon Press.

Okenga, Harold J. Have You Met These Women? Zondervan Publishing.

Olson, R. P. The Reconciled Life, Henderson Publishers, Inc.

Ortlund, Anne. <u>Beautiful Women: A Practical Guide To Spiritual Beauty</u>. Inspirational Press.

Paulk, Norma, <u>Stand by Your Man</u>, Paulk Ministries Books.

Piper & Grudem. <u>Recovering Biblical Manhood & Womanhood</u>. Crossway Books.

Ryrie, Charles Caldwell. <u>The Role of Women in the Church</u>. Moody Press.

Shepherd, Sheri Rose. <u>Fit for Excellence</u>. Creation House Publishing.

Sherrer, Quin & Garlock, Ruthanne. <u>A Woman's Guide to Spiritual Warfare</u>. Vine Books, Ann Arbor, MI, 1991.

Spake, Kluane. <u>From Enmity to Equality</u>. Workforce Press.

Spake, Kluane. <u>Whole & Holy</u>. Workforce Press, 1997.

Spencer, Aida Besancon. <u>Beyond the Curse, Women Called to Ministry</u>. Hendrickson Publishing, 1985.

Swartley, Willard M. <u>Slavery, Sabbath War, & Women</u>. Herald Press, Waterloo, OR, 1983

Tucker, Ruth/Liefeld, Walter. <u>Daughters of the Church</u>. Zondervan Publishing.

Tucker, Ruth. <u>Women in the Maze</u>. Intervarsity Press

Vander Velde, Frances. <u>Women of the Bible</u>. Kregel Publishing.

Weber, Linda. <u>Women of Splendor</u>. Broadman & Holman, Nashville, TN, 1999

TAPE/CD SERIES

Gardner, Rev. Diane, <u>Women of the 21st Century</u>, Vision Publishing

Guerrero, Rev. Cathy <u>Designing Effective Women's Ministries</u>. Vision Publishing

Guerrero, Rev. Cathy. <u>Women of Excellence</u>. Vision Publishing

Hulsey, Dr. Patricia, <u>The Bible and Women</u>. Vision Publishing

Klaus, Dee, Ph.D. <u>Dynamics of Teaching the Word</u>. Vision Publishing

Simpson-Grier, Garnett. <u>History of Women in Ministry</u>. Vision Publishing

Spake, Dr. Kluane, Theology of Women in Ministry, Vision Publishing

www.ingramcontent.com/pod-product-compliance
Lightning Source LLC
Chambersburg PA
CBHW081916170426
43200CB00014B/2742